BATTLEFIELD BRI

THE

Dunacomb
Manrwge
Lee
Duckpoole
Allercomb
Stow
Kilkhamton
Ilcomb
STRATT
ON
Norton
The Meere
Beeds hauen
Poffyll
Stratton Centoorge
Stratton
Lancolls
Efforde
Bynnawy
Thurleher
Borow
Whalsborow
Morkam
Bere
Hilton
Wulston
Langford
Dounfcock
Moris
Trebaffeal
Penfand
Whitston
ALL
Melooke
Dyzade
Penlene
Trefrew
Swanacote
Tamerton
Gennows
Crackington
Iacebstow
Wike
HVN
Vghorot
Boyte
Tintagill Castle
Boscastle
Pulsaoth
Ponallom
Wadefast
Porthceuren Coue
Tintagill
Treuena
Minster
Otterham
Langdon
DRED.
Porisick
Treuillet
Forybery
Treualay
Gillet
Boyton
Trebiarew
Lesnewith
Warpestow
Borden
Lulandyr
Padstow hauen
Helset
Tregargett
Dauidstow
David
Treneglose
stow
Tremene
North petherwyn
Ruscaerrak
Bedwyn
Stuppert poynt
Treuegay
Langelose
Part of Devo Shire
Edithchap
Tresunger
Tre Windle
LESNOWTH
Penhall
Treforo
Sct. Teath
Camelford
Tresmere
Eglosskerry
Trelassc
Polteruoyes
Treberock
Cleibor
Warmington
Endellion
Treburget
Lean cast.
Newheis
Sct. Stephens
Treuorer
Town
Treggget
Lanno
Tigernon
Tamyll
Trewen
Padstow
Prideaux
Mynnuer
Porthilly
Kerw
Tredegy
Advene
Besill
Tregoodock
Newport
Petherick
Michael chap.
Treguit
Michelstowe
Zwallock
Botado
Launston
Trewynon
Buckelly
Berose
Bruard
Foy well
Alternon
Lawhitton
Burnere
Tresmere
Bradstone
Burgus
Bedeuc
S. Tudy
Rowtor
HVNDR ED.
Lawanick
Sct. petherwyn
Treuoura
S. Issie
Tregarden
Trelaske
Eglesshall
Tamsquit
Arthurshall
Betonet
Canalegie
Pellees
Greston
PIDER:
Tredinnick
Mahin
Penpont
Lesante
Breage
Keswell
Penhal
The Moares
Northill
Tredruston
Polmarique
Helega
Trecarrel
Landew
Pawton
Hellan Bridge
Pendre
Tretallock
Blisland
Glyman
Hellan
Temple
EA
ST
Trewullock
HVNDRED.
Caracon Beac
Berio bridg
HVN
Leutham
Trewathe
Dennier Bride
Buckeren
Kilmare
Hurles
Cheswring
Plesh bridg
Sct Wenn
D. Dosmery Poole
Linkinhoin
Stoke
Withiell
Penshereet
Cardinham
Bynethwood
Manniton
Carbullock park
VNDRED.
S. Laurence
Warlegan
Sothill
Castle Anderlas
Pinchecley
Brownwelly
Tretheuy Stones
Brenu
Trengoue
Bodman
Trekene
Trenouth
Kernbridg
Laneuet
Hayes
Lanhetherocock
Sct. Neot
S. Cler
Sct. Benet
Hinkons down
Lepperry
Reptyn
Treworgy
Trebigh
Killitton
Calstock
Roche
Thereck
S. Lue
Bickton
Hensbery
Glynford
Tremaly
Newbrig
Lesterman
Pinock
Cuttcall
ER:
Luxsilton
Listhyell
Lisk erd
Sct. Dominick
Stephens
Ashfelde
Tophowses
Quithock
Lanlyuery
Newton
Polomawgon
Penereck
Tregenall
Crocadon
Towyn
Pill
Minhinet
Pridiausbert
S. Nighton
Brodock
Poole
Trelauke
Hacton
Pillaton
Mownn
S. Blais
Polharma
Boconock
Cayne
Corfether
Laurest
Sct. Melyn
Pelyn
S. Winow
Caynebridg
Clayper bridg
Clifton
Austill
Barrete
Ethye
Wotton
Blosselmin
Cargren
Tresiliam
Trewardreth
Trynhoust
Westnarth
Chaffruch
Polmere
Golanit
Dulo
DRED.
with
Moyale
Port
Premadart
Hiot
Notterbridg
Landilpe
RED.
Colquite
S. Veepe
Sct. Germin
Lawrack
Cargallo
Saltashe
Lanreth
Lanwarnock
Hestonford
S. Stephens
Erne
S. Earth
Shillingham
Polkerres
Comb
Carock passage
Trewargon
Bake
Trinitie
Mcnehsie
Bindon Beacon
Shyvyoke
Trematon
Hall
Plinte
Foye
Langnehan
S. Martyn
Tregonok
W. Antony
Asalt
Lanteglose
East low
Pond
Crostbole
E. Antony
Stonho
Poluan
Trelawn
Sct. Sauiour
Westlowe
Sct. Iohns
Lansallos
Talland
Plimo
Gwyn Rock
Millbrok
Killigath
Polperro
Trewardreth Ba
Sythye Baye
Foye hauene
Maker
S. Michaells Iste
Blackbittle poynte
Rame
Edgcomb
NORTH
nd poynt
ade
aye
outh haue
WEST HVN DRED.

BATTLEFIELD BRITAIN

THE CIVIL WAR IN THE SOUTH-WEST

JOHN BARRATT

First published in Great Britain in 2005 by
PEN & SWORD MILITARY
an imprint of
Pen & Sword Books Ltd
47 Church Street
Barnsley
South Yorkshire
S70 2AS

ISBN: 1-84415-146-8

A CIP catalogue record for this book
is available from the British Library

Edited, designed and typeset (in 9pt Palatino) by Roger Chesneau

Printed in England by CPI UK

Pen & Sword Books Ltd incorporates the imprints of
Pen & Sword Aviation, Pen & Sword Maritime, Pen & Sword Military,
Wharncliffe Local History, Pen and Sword Select, Pen & Sword Military
Classics and Leo Cooper.

For a complete list of Pen & Sword titles please contact:
PEN & SWORD BOOKS LIMITED
47 Church Street, Barnsley, South Yorkshire, S70 2AS, England
E-mail: enquiries@pen-and-sword.co.uk • Website: www.pen-and-sword.co.uk

Frontispiece:
Part of John Speed's map of Cornwall (c.1611). The eastern part
of the county was the scene of bitter fighting on several occasions.

Contents

Preface

The Civil Wars of 1642–51 were a series of conflicts which affected almost every part of the British Isles, dividing communities and spreading destruction across wide areas.

South-west England, despite its distance from centres of power, became caught up in the war from its earliest stages. Though Cornwall in 1642 was largely Royalist in sympathy, and Devon and Somerset predominantly favoured Parliament, in all three counties significant minorities supported the opposing party. The scene was thus set for a bitter struggle which continued for the next four years.

As well as the celebrated exploits of the Cornish Royalist Army in a series of hard-fought engagements, the region also saw, in 1644 and again in 1646, prolonged campaigns by major field armies.

The object of this book is to tell the story of this close-fought struggle and to provide a guide to those wishing to explore in person some of the scenes of these events.

Thanks are due to the staff of various libraries, notably the Sydney Jones Library at the University of Liverpool and the British Library. As always, the team at Pen & Sword have been unfailingly supportive and helpful.

Special thanks are owed to my son, Matthew, whose unflappable driving skills on our field trips more than compensated for my erratic navigational abilities.

John Barratt
September 2004

Introduction

When civil war between King and Parliament broke out in the summer of 1642, most people in the south-west of England shared the general expectation that the conflict would probably be decided quickly by a battle fought in the vicinity of London. It was a hope dashed by the indecisive outcome of the first major engagement of the war, at Edgehill in Warwickshire on 21 October, followed by the King's failure to capture London. During the next few months virtually the whole of England and Wales, followed eventually by Scotland and Ireland, would be drawn into the spreading conflict. Among the first regions to be involved was the south-west of England.

In 1642 there were sharp differences among the three south-western counties of Cornwall, Devon, and Somerset, not only in their political sympathies but also in terms of topography, social factors and economic factors.

As it had for centuries, Cornwall, in the narrowing tip of the south-west peninsula, remained distinctive and apart from much of the mainstream of English life and even from the nearby counties. The Celtic people of Cornwall had remained independent until early in the tenth century, when they had finally been brought under English rule. For centuries, however, Cornwall retained its strongly Celtic character.

In this the Cornish people were aided by geography. Cornwall, until well into modern times, remained comparatively isolated. The River Tamar not only formed the eastern boundary of the county but also emphasised its physical separation. In 1642 three main roads crossed the Tamar into Devon, heading for Plymouth, Tavistock and Okehampton. The Okehampton road crossed the Tamar at Polten Bridge, east of the Cornish town of Launceston, from where it led to the administrative centre of Truro. The Tavistock road entered Cornwall by way of New Bridge near Calstock and went via Liskeard and Lostwithiel to Truro. The third road, from Plymouth, ran via Saltash and Looe to the port of Fowey. Even a century later, Cornish roads were still noted as being amongst the worst in the kingdom, and the county's inaccessibility was increased by its rugged terrain. In 1584 the topographer John Norden described how 'The rocks are high, huge, rugged and craggy, not only upon the sea coast, the Rocks whereof are very high, steep and hard, but also the inland mountains are crowned with mighty rock.'

This wild and rugged terrain, with its little ports and rocky, cliff-bound coves, and, inland, a network of small, high-banked and hedged fields rising towards the wilds of Bodmin Moor, had helped preserve a Cornish sense of separateness. This was symbolised by the Cornish language. In steady retreat for over 500 years, by 1642 Cornish was still widely spoken only in the area to the west of Truro, though the majority of Cornish-speakers could also understand English. It was mainly a language of the poor, who were 'laughed at by the rich, because they understand it not.'

Cornwall's physical isolation, and the ever-present reminders of its ancient past, had helped to breed a spirit of independence and recklessness among its people. During Tudor times large numbers of Cornish had on three occasions risen in rebellion for a variety of motives, underlying all of which had been the fear that their ancient way of life was under terminal threat from across the Tamar. Many of the Cornish gentry and their retainers had been privateers and pirates (the distinction was often blurred) during Elizabeth's long war with Spain.

For many, perhaps the majority, of Cornwall's people, life was a hard and unremitting struggle for existence. True, from the point of view of those involved in farming and fishing, it was still more the case for the thousands of Cornish tin miners, relatively few of whom could be expected to reach old age.

The harshness of many peoples' lives, as well as physical isolation, had a marked effect on the nature of Cornish society. Since at least Tudor times the Cornish were viewed with a mixture of alarm and distrust by the rest of the English population. Whilst admitting to their proven ability in war — in the 1630s Cornwall was said to be 'prolific in the most warlike men of the Kingdom' — Englishmen regarded the Cornish as an alien, potentially treacherous people. This dislike and suspicion was returned with interest.

Cornish society remained intensely parochial, its families closely linked by intermarriage. Even the gentry, who generally received part of their education in Oxford, Cambridge or London and frequently travelled widely at home and abroad, still tended to marry at home. Cornish society was also strongly conservative. It had a growing if still relatively small merchant class, but its towns remained modest in size and were mainly dependent on the tin and overseas trade, both of which were in decline during the decade prior to the Civil War. Much of the land in the county was owned by the Crown through the Duchy of Cornwall, and the tin trade was a royal monopoly, albeit one administered — with a wide overspill into other aspects of Cornish life — by the semi-autonomous Stannary Courts. Many Cornish people were tenants of the Duchy, which had proved a relatively good, if conservative, landlord.

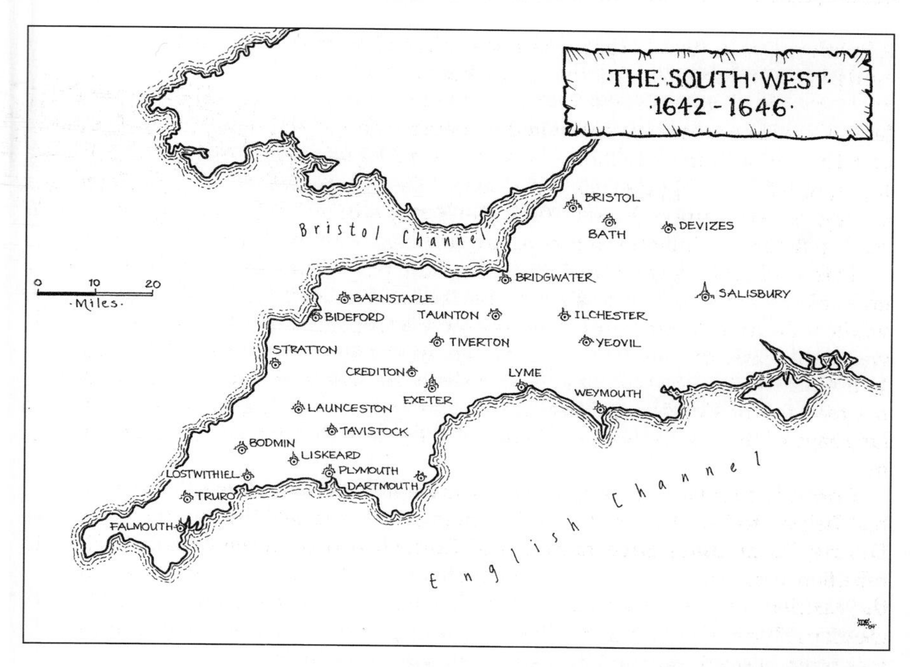

Its approach was echoed by many of the Cornish gentry. Their relationship with their tenants and retainers still had the feudal overtones that were fast disappearing elsewhere in England. In 1644 the Royalist Sir Edward Walker wrote approvingly that the Cornish gentry 'retain their old possessions, their old tenants and expect from them their ancient reverence and obedience.'

Cornish views on religious and political affairs echoed this innate conservatism. Most people remained Anglican in belief, though there were a small number of Puritans, mainly in the towns. However, a natural tendency to favour the monarchy did not prevent the strong streak of Cornish independence leading to friction during the period of Charles I's 'Personal Rule' in the 1630s. Many of the Duchy's MPs, notably Sir John Eliot, were persistent opponents of perceived royal excesses.

However, in the political polarisation which followed the outbreak of the Bishops' Wars at the end of the decade, Cornish traditionalism increasingly displayed itself by rallying to the Royalist cause. Sir Bevil Grenville, perhaps the most influential of the Cornish gentry, explained his decision to fight for the King in the First Bishops' War by saying, 'I cannot contain myself within my doors when the King of England's standard waves in the field upon so just occasion.' The process was hastened by the impeachment and trial, in 1641, of the King's chief minister, the Earl of Strafford. Eight Cornish MPs, later among the most prominent of the Cornish Royalists, voted against the Attainder of Strafford.

Although the majority of the Cornish gentry — and, by extension, their tenants and other dependants — favoured the Royalist cause, their view was not universally held in Cornwall. In the summer of 1642 there remained a significant pro-Parliament

The Cornish Image

The sense of separateness common among many of the Cornish people was not due solely to their geographical isolation. Celtic Cornwall had remained independent until the tenth century, and both a historical awareness and the declining Cornish language- increasingly confined to the western parts of the county- conformed the Cornish sense of being a people apart from the mainstream of English life.

This independence was graphically demonstrated by a series of rebellions in the fifteenth and mid-sixteenth centuries, one result of which was that Cornwall continued to be regarded by English governments as a potential area of disloyalty and sedition. There was also a more general feeling of dislike and contempt directed towards the Cornish people as a whole: 'a poor realm and a boorish [one]' or a 'wild spot where [no one] ever comes, save the few boors who inhabit it'. In 1628 even Sir John Eliot, a prominent Cornishman who was one of the leaders of the Parliamentary opposition to Charles I wrote about 'the ignorance of these Cornish parts, almost as much divided from reason and intelligence as their island is from the rest of the world'.

Whilst Queen Elizabeth I is said to have remarked that 'Cornish gentlemen are all born courtiers, with a becoming confidence', her view remained an exception. Among most of those living east of the Tamar, 'Cornish choughs' was used as a derogatory term.

party, headed by the Puritan Lord Robartes. Until one party or the other secured control of the towns and the militia, Cornwall's final choice of allegiance remained uncertain.

The county of Devon, Cornwall's neighbour to the east of the Tamar, was a marked contrast. It had wild, remote upland areas such as Dartmoor and Exmoor but, as a contemporary explained, it was 'altogether for the most part wild, full of wastes, heaths and moors, uphill and downhill amongst the rocks and stones.' However, traversed by a number of major rivers, including the Exe, Dart and Tore, Devon contained much rich agricultural land. It was England's third largest county and one of the wealthiest, with a population of about 227,000. Its principal towns were Exeter, with some 10,000 inhabitants, and the major port of Plymouth, with slightly fewer people. Other important settlements were Tiverton, Dartmouth, Bideford and Barnstaple.

During the years before the Civil War, Devon's principal occupation — farming — was expanding. The county had few great magnates owning land within its borders: the bulk of the land was owned or farmed by minor gentry and by yeoman and tenant farmers. Some mining for tin and other ores was carried on, though much less than in Cornwall, but fishing was equally as important as in the neighbouring county, especially for coastal towns such as Dartmouth. In the northern and eastern parts of Devon the woollen industry led to the rise of significant mercantile interests. The main influence of the merchants was, however, confined to the towns. In the rural areas power lay with the landed gentry, if not to quite the same extent as in Cornwall. The majority of them were small landowners, each with a handful of tenants – perhaps around 50 families on average. A large proportion of the population was tied to the land, either as tenant farmers or agricultural labourers.

During the early years of the reign of Charles I, Devon's long-term prosperity had suffered a number of setbacks. The county was afflicted by plague, whilst Plymouth felt the adverse effects of the King's foreign policy and his unsuccessful military expeditions to Cadiz and La Rochelle. Plymouth was the main base for both of these, and maintaining the large numbers of disorderly troops raised for these campaigns placed a heavy burden on the county. Whilst still weighed down by this burden, Devonians were hit by the King's demands for forced loans. The trade of Devon's ports suffered as a result of piracy, particularly the activities of the Barbary corsairs whose raids afflicted the Western Approaches to the English Channel. Whilst the coastal areas might see the relevance of the levy of 'Ship Money', purportedly raised to strengthen the Navy, for the inland inhabitants of Devon, like the rest of England, this was yet another unjustified burden placed on them. By the late 1630s there were increasing numbers of cases coming before the courts of individuals refusing to pay.

A rapid growth in Devon's population was worsening the economic difficulties, and the result was steadily increasing discontent which sought religious and political outlets. There was already a significant Puritan population within the county, and the outbreak of the Bishop's Wars in 1638 provided a focus for opposition. There was also concern about the increased powers which Charles had reserved for the Crown, many ordinary people sharing the opinion of Devonian Francis Buller, who pondered, 'Though our king be gracious and just: others after him may not: therefore things must be so settled that when kings shall not be well minded they may not do much hurt.'

By the end of the decade the majority of influential men within Devon favoured some degree of political and religious reform, though differing over its extent. An edge was added to their concern by the outbreak of rebellion in Ireland in 1641. This rekindled the fear of Catholicism that had been a feature of popular anxieties since the time of the Spanish Armada, and alarm was heightened by the lurid tales brought by the English refugees from Ireland who made their landfall at the north Devon ports. One result was that a number of Devon merchants provided funding for the suppression of the Irish rebellion: its defeat would not only safeguard Devon from Irish Catholic invasion but also provide the speculators with a handsome profit. As the King was popularly (if inaccurately) suspected of siding with the Irish rebels, the sympathies of many influential people in Devon consequently rested with Parliament.

Nonetheless, as civil war approached in the summer of 1642, most of Devon's inhabitants still hoped that the conflict might pass them by. In the event, forced into making a choice by the attempts of Royalist Commissioners of Array to raise troops in the county, most of the merchants and gentry of the county sided with Parliament, which gained overall control in the county. There remained significant Royalist support, especially among some of the gentry, but it would require outside assistance before it could come into the open.

The final county within our area was Somerset. It was noted as a fertile land, with a number of fine towns and great houses, often built from the profits of the woollen trade. A notable topographical feature was the large areas of marshland in the centre of the county, which, along with a number of rivers and the Mendip Hills in the east, formed barriers to easy travel not always improved by the county's averagely maintained roads. Although it contained several small ports, such as Minehead and Bridgwater on the northern coast, and a number of thriving market towns, such as Taunton, Chard and Yeovil, Somerset remained primarily a rural county. There were a number of minor industries — quarrying and lead mining in the Mendips and woollen manufacture in many of the towns — but agriculture remained as the predominant occupation.

Like Devon, Somerset had suffered major economic depression during the decade prior to the Civil War, and this had fuelled discontent with the royal government. Somerset faced the same problems of overpopulation and unemployment as other areas, but, even more than in Devon, religious concerns played an important role. Many of the cloth workers, in particular, were Puritans, and the outbreak of the religiously motivated Bishops' Wars led to widespread discontent in Somerset, including mutiny among some of the levies conscripted there. Significantly, John Pym, a leading figure in the Parliamentary opposition to King Charles, was a Somerset man, and his views were shared by many of his former neighbours.

By the summer of 1642 popular discontent was finding expression in increasing numbers of attacks and vandalism aimed at churches in the county, identified with the unpopular religious reforms of the King and Archbishop Laud. Many of the leading county magnates were Royalist, but they faced massive popular opposition, especially from among the cloth workers. On 11 July tensions finally came to a head when Charles ordered his nominated General in the West, William Seymour, Marquis of Hertford, to issue his Commission of Array in Somerset and begin raising troops for the King's army. On 19 July, in a direct challenge, the local Parliamentarian leader, Sir Alexander Popham, was ordered by Westminster to put Parliament's Militia Ordnance into effect and bring out the Somerset levies for Parliament.

Civil War had come to Somerset, and soon would engulf the whole of the south-west of England.

Chapter I

The Early Battles, 1642–43

Few people ever credited William Seymour, Marquis of Hertford, with being a great soldier. Indeed, the Earl of Clarendon, who knew Hertford, opined that the king's newly appointed Lieutenant General in the West was 'not fit for much activity and fatigue, and wedded so to his ease that he loved his book above all exercises.' Hertford, Governor to the Prince of Wales, was typical of the 'grandee' appointments — men chosen more for their social and financial status and local influence than for any military experience — common among Royalist regional commanders in the early stages of the war.

On arriving in Somerset, Hertford was fortunate in securing as his field marshal, or second in command, a leading Somerset Royalist, Sir Ralph Hopton. Hopton had some previous Continental military experience, and would prove himself to be a usually, though not invariably, competent commander. But even a more able general than Hertford would have found the odds stacked against him in Somerset in 1642. Though the majority of the

William Seymour, Marquis of Hertford (1588–1660). One of the 'grandees' appointed to senior command by the King early in the war because of his status and influence rather than because of proven military ability, Hertford generally seems to have followed the advice of more experienced soldiers.

Ralph, Lord Hopton (1598–1652)
Hopton was a member of a Somerset gentry family that had served with the Protestant forces on the Continent during the early part of the Thirty Years' War. Here he became a friend of Sir William Waller, his long-standing opponent during the Civil War. Active in local and national affairs before the war, Hopton was a moderate opponent of the King until he turned Royalist in reaction to the growing radicalism of Parliament's aims. In 1642 he was appointed second in command to the Marquis of Hertford.

Frequently overrated by historians, Hopton was in fact a competent if unimaginative commander.

Somerset gentry nominally supported the Royalist cause, the smaller number of Parliamentarian sympathisers were both more active and better organised. Hertford never really recovered from his initial mistake in establishing his headquarters at Wells rather than at the far more important city of Bristol, and was unable to muster more than a few hundred men, compared with several thousand raised by his Parliamentarian opponent, Francis Russell, Earl of Bedford.

Although Bedford was hardly more capable than Hertford, he at least had an overwhelming numerical advantage. The Royalists won an unimportant skirmish at Marshall's Elm (4 August), but two days later they withdrew to the stronghold of Sherbourne Castle in Dorset, where they remained for six weeks, effectively ceding control of Somerset to Parliament. This outcome was confirmed by a minor Royalist reverse at Babylon Hill in which Hopton narrowly escaped capture, and Hertford, viewing the situation as hopeless, headed for the small port of Minehead on the Bristol Channel, intending to ship his little force over to Royalist-held south Wales.

At this point — though Sir Ralph tactfully minimises it in his own account — there was a difference of opinion among the Royalist commanders. The outcome was that while Hertford and his few hundred infantry followed his original plan and crossed into south Wales, Hopton, with about 110 horse and dragoons, remained behind. Their options were limited. Somerset and Devon were firmly in Parliamentarian hands, and Bedford's forces could block any attempt by Hopton to march to join the King, now on the Welsh border. Significantly, Hopton's little force was accompanied by several prominent Cornish Royalist leaders, and it was probably at their urging that Hopton decided to head westwards in an attempt to secure Cornwall for the King.

The situation west of the Tamar was not necessarily encouraging for them. Cornwall remained divided in its sympathies. In August supporters of both parties put their cases to the county assizes in Launceston, and thanks to the support of the Sheriff, John Grylls, the Royalists gained a precarious upper hand. This was not, however, translated into popular enthusiasm, and throughout August recruiting attempts by both sides met with little response, partly perhaps because bringing in the harvest was of more immediate concern. On 17 August an attempted muster organised at Bodmin by Sir Bevil Grenville raised only 150 men, and the blue and white spirals painted on their pike staffs and musket rests proclaimed them as Grenville's own tenants and retainers.

The Parliamentarians were meeting with no more success, and it was probably because of this that a fifteen-day local truce was agreed on 18 August.

This uneasy lull was still continuing on 25 September, when Hopton and his small force arrived at Grenville's family home at Stowe near Stratton in north Cornwall. The events which followed were probably orchestrated largely by Grenville and his Cornish Royalist associates, with Hopton and his horse providing the armed force necessary to tip the fragile balance. The Cornish Parliamentarians reacted to Hopton's arrival by calling a muster of the Cornish Trained Bands for 28 September at Bodmin to oppose the Royalist arrivals. It was clearly necessary for Hopton and Grenville to pre-empt this move, and on 27 September they reached Bodmin, causing the small Cornish Parliamentarian force under Sir Richard Buller to retire to Launceston.

With the Trained Band Muster for the moment thwarted, Hopton headed for Truro, where the County Assizes was holding its Michaelmas session. What followed was probably carefully orchestrated beforehand. A Cornish Royalist leader, Sir Richard Vyvyan, addressed a crowd gathered outside the town hall, calling on them assist their sheriff and justices in proclaiming the king's Commission of Array. A carefully primed assizes jury listened to Hopton's justification for bringing armed men into Cornwall, and not only acquitted him but thanked him for his efforts!

Sir Bevil Grenville (1596–1643)

An influential figure in Cornwall, and an MP, Grenville had limited military experience in the First Scots War. He is generally regarded as the epitome of the dedicated Royalist, as expressed in his comment when pledging his support for the King during that war: 'I cannot contain myself within my doors when the King of England's standard waves in the field upon so just an occasion, the cause being such as must make all those that die in it little inferior to martyrs.' In fact, until that point he had been a moderate opponent of the King's policies.

A patron of the arts, who admitted that at Oxford University he 'fell upon the sweet delights of reading poetry and history . . . and troubled no other book, and do find myself so infinitely defective by it, as I would give a limb it were otherwise', Grenville was portrayed by Clarendon as being universally loved. In practice he was a strict but fair landlord, and the moving force of the Cornish Royalists.

The Armies

The armies involved in the war for the West, though frequently smaller than those engaged in other parts of the country, were organised along the same lines. The cavalry, or 'horse', were still regarded as the dominant force on the battlefield. The ideal cavalry trooper was protected by back and breast plates and a variation of the 'pot' helmet. He was armed with a sword, a pair of pistols and a short-barrelled carbine. Cavalry tactics evolved in the course of the war from the sedate 'caracole', in which horse relied primarily on firepower to disorganise the ranks of their opponents, to shock methods in which cavalry advanced briskly at a 'good round trot' and at the most fired one pistol before closing with their opponents in hand-to-hand combat.

In an ideal infantry unit, two-thirds of its men would be musketeers and the remainder pikemen, though frequently, particularly early in the war, the proportion of the latter would be higher. Most of the musketeers were armed with the matchlock — a cheap and easily operated musket — though it was unreliable in wet or windy weather, when the length of match soaked in gunpowder and resin used to fire it was often extinguished. A reasonably proficient musketeer could fire three or four shots a minute, though in hand-to-hand combat most preferred to employ their musket in the role of a club.

The pikeman had originally worn full body armour, though this was rarely issued during the Civil War. He was armed with a sword and a 16-foot-long pike, frequently shortened by three or four feet for ease of handling. His main role was to defend the musketeers against enemy cavalry, and to engage his opposite numbers in a kind of pushing 'rugby scrum' known as 'push of pike'.

Dragoons, commonly employed by Civil War armies, were a variety of mounted infantry, armed with carbines, who commonly fought on foot and were employed for skirmishing, for reconnaissance and, frequently, as raiders or convoy escorts.

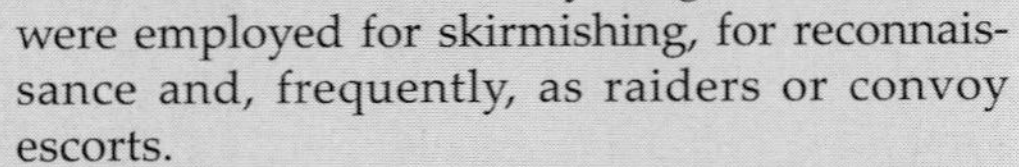

The main use of artillery was in siege warfare, although guns heavy enough to be really effective in this role were both difficult to transport and greedy in their demands for gunpowder. Lighter pieces, with a bewildering variety of names and sizes, were sometimes employed in battle, although generally with a fairly limited effect. In the West they seem to have played a significant role only at Langport in 1645.

At the start of the war few soldiers on either side received uniform dress. Often, like the musketeer shown here, they wore assorted items of civilian dress, with individual regiments perhaps distinguished by coloured ribbons. Note the tin powder chargers, the matchlock musket and the cheap sword.

Their legal position assured, on 4 October Hopton and the Cornish Royalists called a muster on nearby Moilesbarrow Down of the *posse comitatus*, theoretically consisting of all fit men in the county between the ages of sixteen and sixty. In practice about 3,000 men, mostly from the western part of Cornwall, turned out. Ill-armed and poorly disciplined though they were, they enabled Hopton to march on Launceston, whence the Cornish Parliamentarians hastily retired across the Tamar into Devon.

Raising the Armies

The Royalists might have gained control of Cornwall, but they lacked an adequate force with which to defend their hold or extend it. A portent of trouble came when the unruly militia sacked a number of houses in Launceston, forcing Hopton to imprison about twenty of them. Buller, with about 700 men, had withdrawn to Plymouth, and although Hopton managed to secure Saltash, on the Cornish side of the Tamar opposite Plymouth, he lacked the legal authority to take the Cornish Trained Bands outside the county, even if they had been willing to go, which they were not.

It was clearly essential to raise a 'volunteer' army, which might be willing to operate without such restrictions. The King had, in August, already set up a temporary command structure for his western forces in the absence of Hertford, who retained the post of general. Hopton was lieutenant general of horse, Sir John Berkeley was commissary general and William Ashburnham major general of foot. None of the three was a Cornishman, and the arrangement might seem to have discriminated against the Cornish Royalist commanders. In practice, arrangements seem to have been a good deal more blurred, with three of the Cornish Royalist commanders in the army now being raised exercising a good deal of influence.

As well as Sir Bevil Grenville, the other leading Cornish military activists were Sir Nicholas Slanning and John Trevanion. Slanning was a prominent figure in Cornwall, and a leading figure in the tin trade. A man of 'a sharp and discerning wit, a staid and stolid judgement', he was described as the 'life and soul' of the Cornish forces. As well as raising a

Sir Nicholas Slanning (1606–43). Another leading figure in Cornwall, Slanning was an MP and served in the First Scots War, and also held a command in the Cornish Trained Bands. His involvement in the tin trade resulted in large numbers of miners being recruited for his Regiment.

John Trevanyon (c.1606–43). A friend of Slanning and Grenville, Trevanyon was another of the charismatic commanders who providHe was kKilled with Slanning at the storming of Bristol.

regiment of foot, partly from among the tin miners, Slanning would play a leading role in organising the sale of tin on the Continent, purchasing munitions with the proceeds. He also had some pre-war military experience in Europe. Trevanion was aged twenty-nine on the outbreak of war, and had been an MP in the pre-war Parliament. An evidently charismatic character, he too would raise a regiment of foot for the Cornish Army.

A more ambivalent role was played by a fourth founding figure of the Cornish Army. Warwick, 3rd Lord Mohun, with his seat at Boconnoc, near Lostwithiel, was one of the few Cornish peers. He seems initially to have hoped to avoid any involvement in the war, and unsuccessfully attempted to slip away to London. Thwarted in this, by virtue of his position Mohun raised a regiment of foot for the Cornish Army, 'though he had not the good fortune to be very gracious', and opted out of active personal involvement as quickly as possible.

Throughout October work continued on raising the new force, based at Bodmin. By the end of the month Hopton felt that he had 'some reasonable show of an Army', although at this stage he could still only muster about 1,500 foot and five light guns to add to his original small force of horse.

As with other units raised by both sides, the term 'volunteer', when used to describe the Cornish regiments, is somewhat misleading. The Cornish units, like those recruited in similar circumstances in parts of Wales, were noted for their strong local connections. In the five foot regiments which formed the basis of Hopton's Cornish Army, most of the officers, apart from a few Devon men, were from Cornwall, usually relatives of their colonels or other minor gentry or yeoman farmers. The bulk of the rank and file were connected with, or dependent in some way upon, their officers, either as tenants or employees. As a result, their degree of choice in enlisting was usually distinctly limited. Parliamentarian accounts said of Sir Bevil Grenville, usually regarded as a benevolent landlord, whose foot regiment was the first to reach its established strength of 1,200, 'Sir Bevil Grenville hath been a tyrant, especially to his tenants, threatening to thrust them out of house and home if they will not assist him and his confederates.

There was an echo of this accusation in a letter from Grenville to his wife, Grace, complaining that a number of his neighbours had failed to respond to the initial call to arms issued by the Sheriff of Cornwall:

> My neighbours did ill that they came not out, and are punishable by law in high degree; and though I will do the best I can to save some of the honester sort, yet others shall smart.

> My neighbours did perchance look to hear from me, and if we proceed I shall expect they should yet come forth, or they shall suffer . . .

The impression often given by writers, echoing Clarendon, that the Cornish Army was a kind of 'Band of Brothers', united and inspired by bonds of loyalty, needs to be viewed with caution. Certainly many of the officers were brought together by family connections and the common interests of their class, but the attitudes of their followers were more mixed. The sometimes ambivalent ties between landlord and tenant were critical. Four of the foot regiments were recruited mainly on, and in the neighbourhood of, their commanders' estates. In Grenville's Regiment, for example, all but one of the officers came from Grenville's home area of north-east Cornwall, and eight of John Trevanion's officers are known to be from around his estates in the south and centre of the county. Two other colonels, Sir Nicholas Slanning and William Godolphin, had extensive tin mining interests, and most of their men seem to have been miners.

Of the colonels, only Slanning, and to a lesser extent Grenville, had any previous military experience. The same pattern may be found among their subordinates. In Grenville's Regiment, only his Major, George Lower, had definitely seen previous service. Most officers of the five volunteer regiments seem to have been amateurs, and the same was true of most of their men, apart from those with some theoretical military knowledge from service with the Trained Bands and those who had served with Grenville and Slanning in the relatively bloodless Bishops' Wars.

That many of the men did serve primarily out of loyalty to their commanders and in solidarity with their local communities is certain. However, this can be exaggerated, as is perhaps confirmed by the slow progress in raising recruits and the frequently mutinous behaviour of the soldiers.

In practice, even if recruits had come in more rapidly, Hopton would initially have found it very difficult to support them. The Cornish colonels themselves at first had to pay for the upkeep of their regiments, assisted by contributions of money and plate from the other loyalist Cornish gentry. Their equipment was equally inadequate, the recruits initially being armed 'partly out of the Gentlemen's particular stores, and partly out of those that belonged to the Trained Bands of the county'. But the quantity of arms, ammunition and powder obtained was inadequate. It was probably a long time before the recruits received any kind of uniform, continuing to wear their own civilian clothes and with the different regiments distinguished by coloured ribbons.

It would take some time for Hopton's more urgent needs to be eased. Sir Francis Bassett and Nicholas Slanning were put in charge of importing munitions from the Continent, paid for by the proceeds of the tin trade, into the Cornish ports of Falmouth, St Ives and Penzance. Slanning also organised ships to act as privateers, preying on allegedly Parliamentarian merchant shipping. Although the Parliamentarian fleet had overall superiority at sea, it proved unable to stifle the Royalist vessels, despite some successes, such as the incident in November 1642 when a ship was intercepted carrying 300 muskets, five light guns and 500 cases of pistols as well as a kinsman of Sir Bevil Grenville who had been employed by him to purchase arms supplies in France.

The Royalists' preparations for war were matched by the Parliamentarians' efforts to the east of the Tamar. Hopton's success in securing Cornwall for the King meant that Parliament's hold on Devon was likely to come under threat, and Westminster reacted by authorising the refugee Cornish Parliamentarian leadership to raise 1,000 men as well as commissioning several volunteer regiments in other parts of the county. The Devon Parliamentary Committee saw its immediate priorities as securing and strengthening the defences of Exeter, Plymouth and the north Devon ports, suppressing Royalist support, particularly in the south of Devon, and eventually taking the offensive into Cornwall.

On 17 October the leading gentry of the county were ordered to provide funds for the defence of Devon, and further soldiers, including a troop of horse and a company of dragoons, were to be raised, with the combined forces of Devon and its neighbours to the east, as far as the Isle of Wight, coming under the nominal command of the Earl of Pembroke. More reinforcements, including seven troops of horse and 1,000 foot, under the Earl of Bedford, were also on their way.

Pembroke, however, proved to be an inactive commander. Fortunately for the citizens of Plymouth — likely to be the first place threatened by the Royalists — they received a fortuitous reinforcement when a contingent of troops raised by a Scottish professional soldier, Colonel William Ruthven, intending to take employment on the Continent, were driven into the port by bad weather and decided to offer their services to Parliament.

Early in November, though his forces were still not complete, Hopton, after some indecisive skirmishing with Ruthven's men out of Plymouth and encouraged by promises of support from the Devon Royalists, moved eastwards across the Tamar. His 'volunteers' proved, however, no more eager to leave their native county than had the Trained Bands, and had to be bribed with an advance of pay.

Partly because of prompt countermeasures by the Parliamentarians, Hopton's anticipated support from the Devon Royalists failed to materialise, and, although he was able to chase Ruthven back into Plymouth and occupy Tavistock, the Royalist commander had no more substantial success to claim. Urged on by further promises of support, the Cornish Army advanced on Exeter, which Hopton had been assured would surrender without a fight. However, on arriving before Exeter on 18 November, Hopton found his summons firmly rejected, and, after an exchange of artillery fire, the Cornishmen were sufficiently roughly handled in a sally by the defenders to abandon their attempt and pull back to Tavistock.

With more optimism than solid grounds for confidence, Hopton turned his attention to Plymouth, and, with his headquarters at Plympton, established a number of outposts to blockade the town on its landward side. Some indecisive skirmishes followed, with Ruthven, by now being reinforced and supplied by sea, making initially unsuccessful attempts to break the Royalist blockade. Still hoping for support from Devon, Hopton and the Royalist High Sheriff of the county called upon the *posse commitatus* to muster at Modbury on 6 December. As was usually the case, only a few men appeared, and these, according to Hopton, were 'so transported with the jollity of the thing that no man was capable of the labour, care and discipline'.

This jovial gathering was too good an opportunity for Ruthven to miss, and in a dawn sortie on 7 December he quickly dispersed the militia, Hopton, according to

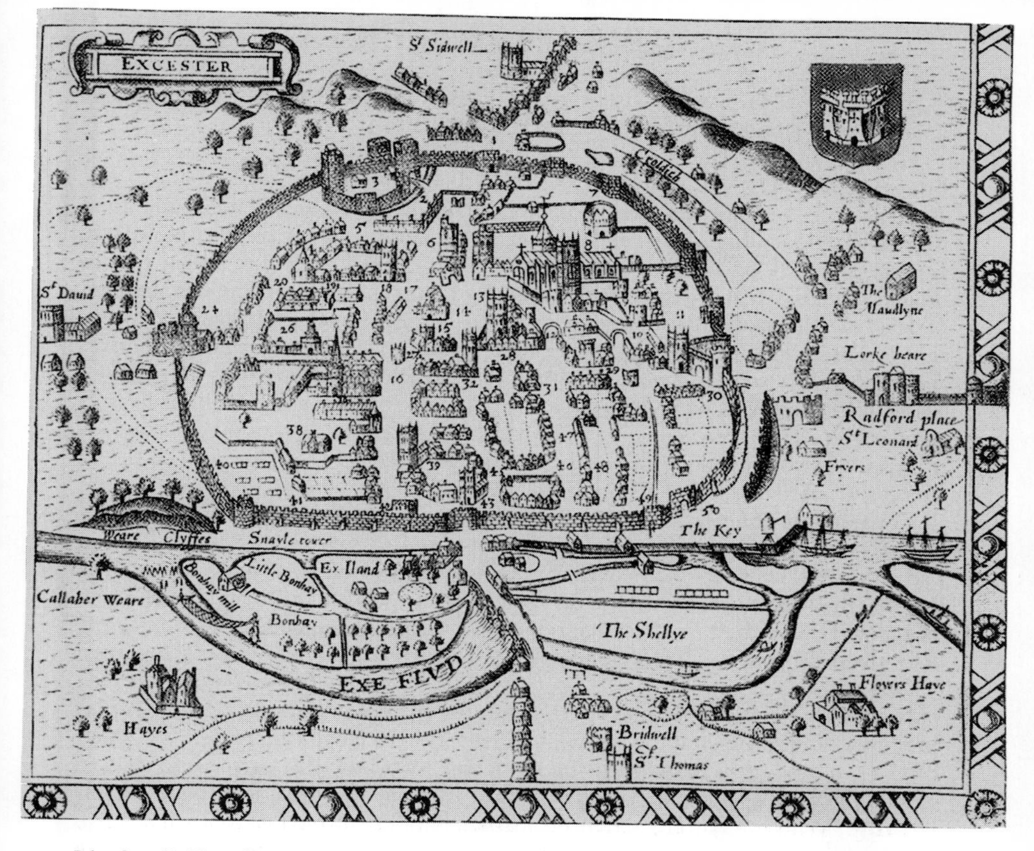

John Speed's Plan of Exeter (c.1611). The city's medieval defences were strengthened with more modern fortifications during the war.

one account, narrowly escaping capture. His designs on Plymouth thwarted, Hopton withdrew to Totnes in largely pro-Royalist south Devon, and pillaged the surrounding countryside. The Parliamentarians meanwhile were strengthening the defences of Barnstaple in north Devon and raising troops in the area to combat a Royalist force mustering at Torrington.

Just before Christmas, again optimistically believing hints of local Royalist assistance, Hopton made a renewed advance on Exeter. He was once more disappointed with the outcome. The Cornish lacked the strength fully to blockade the city, which had been reinforced from Plymouth by Ruthven. After a half-hearted assault had been repulsed on 1 January, the Royalists retreated slowly westwards, 'in that bitter season of the year', as Hopton ruefully put it . As they trudged back towards the Tamar, via Crediton, Okehampton and Bridestowe, the sullen Cornish foot were 'through the whole march so disobedient and mutinous, as little service was expected of them if they should be attempted by the Enemy.' Despite Hopton's fears, however, when a party of Parliamentarian horse approached near Bridestowe, the Cornishmen promptly fell into rank and saw them off.

By 4 January 1643 the Royalist army was back in Cornwall at Launceston, its first invasion of Devon having ended in ignominious failure.

Braddock Down

The initiative now passed to the Parliamentarians. Reinforcements, including three regiments of foot, under a new and more energetic commander, the Earl of Stamford, were on the way, and these reached Exeter on 6 January. Stamford's plan was to unite his forces with those under Ruthven at Plymouth and, with a combined strength of 4,500 men, cross the Tamar and destroy the Cornish Royalists. Instructions were sent by Parliament for additional funds to be raised in Devon to support this force.

The Royalists were in a poor condition to meet the imminent threat of invasion. Many of their troops were mutinous through lack of pay, and lacked arms and ammunition. They were saved by a mixture of blunders by their opponents and an unexpected stroke of good luck. Ruthven, possibly anxious to capitalise on his initial success or, as is sometimes suggested, wishing to gain credit for defeating the Royalists before Stamford arrived, attacked the crossing of the Tamar at Newbridge with a mixed force of troops, including units from Dorset, Somerset and Devon, and a small Cornish Parliamentarian regiment of foot under Francis Buller. The Royalists had broken down the arches of the bridge, but whilst Ruthven's musketeers exchanged fire with its Royalist defenders his horse and dragoons crossed at a ford below the bridge, chasing off a small group of enemy dragoons and capturing three or four of them.

Next morning, probably after effecting temporary repairs to the bridge, the Parliamentarian force crossed into Cornwall. In response the Royalist garrison of Saltash abandoned the town and withdrew through Launceston to join Hopton's main force at Bodmin. Ruthven himself crossed by boat from Plymouth to join his troops at Saltash, bringing with him reinforcements, including Carew's Cornish horse and his own Scots professional soldiers. Probably hastened by news of the Earl of Stamford's imminent arrival at Plymouth, he pushed on to Liskeard.

At this point, what the Royalists would claim as the workings of Providence intervened on Hopton's behalf. On 17 January stormy weather forced three Parliamentarian ships, laden with arms and ammunition — and, equally importantly, money — to seek shelter in Falmouth, where they were promptly seized by the exultant Royalists. With their contents, and £204 rapidly raised by Francis Bassett, Hopton was able to re-equip his men and provide them with all their pay arrears plus an additional fortnight's wages

Henry Grey, 1st Earl of Stamford (1599–1673). Though having little previous military experience, Stamford was an energetic commander, but found himself outmatched by Hopton.

Braddock Down from the south. The Royalist forces were deployed on the left, roughly along the line of the hedges. Ruthven's Parliamentarians were on the rising ground on the right. The Royalists advanced across the dip in the ground between the two ridges.

in advance. A rendezvous was called the same day at Moilesborrow Down, where the five volunteer foot regiments, with a few horse and dragoons and some of the Cornish Trained Bands and *posse comitatus* were gathered, making a total of about 5,000 men.

Refreshed and revived, the Royalist Council of War met on 18 January at Lord Mohun's house at Boconnoc, where their troops spent the night encamped in the park. The Council decided that their only hope lay in engaging Ruthven before he could be reinforced by Stamford, and around noon on 19 January the Royalists set off in search of the enemy.

As Hopton's men crested the hill above Boconnoc, their scouts sighted the enemy drawn up on rising ground on the eastern side of Braddock Down, just to the west of the present-day village of East Taphouse. The terrain consisted of two areas of heathland, with a few enclosures and areas of shrubs. Several prehistoric tumuli formed prominent features.

Both commanders seem to have been slightly surprised by the encounter. Ruthven had left Liskeard that morning, heading for Lostwithiel, and apparently believed the enemy to be in retreat. His march had been slowed by 'narrow and very dirty lanes' and, despite having Cornish Parliamentarians with him, he seems to have found difficulty in obtaining accurate information regarding the locality and Royalist movements. The Parliamentarian commander claimed later that he had been surprised when Hopton's men emerged from the woods above Boconnoc, and after some skirmishing between opposing horse and dragoons the Parliamentarians fell back to the ridge just short of East Taphouse, and both sides began to deploy for battle.

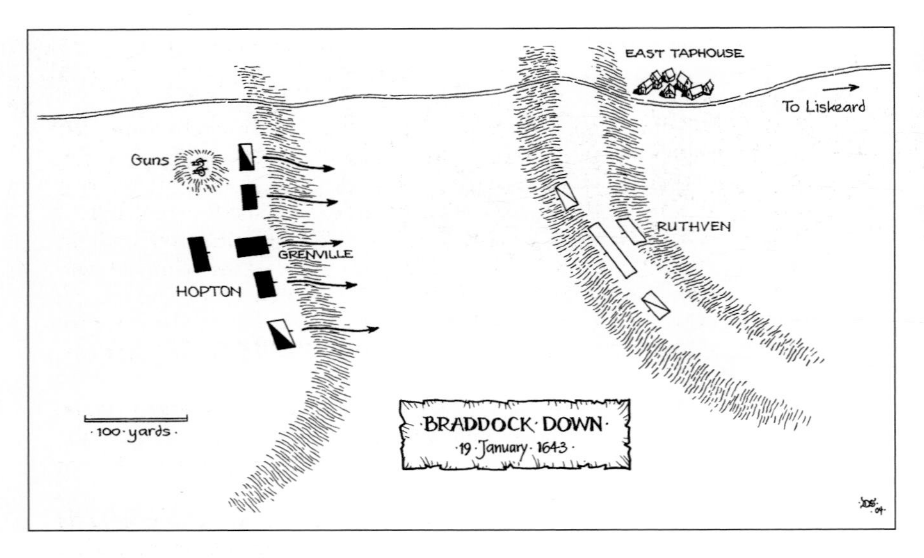

The Royalists had simplified their confused command structure by requesting Hopton to command during the battle, and he drew up his forces on the west side of Braddock Down 'in the best order he could'. He had a slight advantage in numbers, with perhaps 5,000 men against a Parliamentarian force of 3–4,000. Both armies included troops of widely varying quality.

Hopton advanced a party of musketeers to line the hedges of some small enclosures to the front of his main position and drew up his body of foot on the ridge itself, in two lines, with horse and dragoons stationed on his flanks. The Parliamentarians, who probably had a slight numerical advantage in horse over Hopton's 250 troopers, deployed in similar fashion on the north-east side of Braddock Down, keeping a reserve of foot in the hedges behind their main position.

The opposing forces were within musket shot of each other, and neither at first showed any desire to quit their strong position and launch an attack. About two hours of largely ineffectual exchanges of musket fire between the opposing forlorn-hopes in the hedgerows followed, until Hopton decided to take the initiative.

Two light guns, or drakes, belonging to Lord Mohun were dragged up the hill from Boconnoc and advanced within range of the enemy, concealed behind a party of horse. With the Parliamentarian artillery still bogged down in the lanes leading from Liskeard, Hopton decided to launch a general assault.

Prayers were said at the head of the divisions of foot and then, after the drakes had fired a couple of rounds, the Cornish foot advanced down one slope and up the other towards the Parliamentarian position. The assault was headed by Sir Bevil Grenville's Regiment of Foot, with the less reliable Trained Bands and militia in support. The horse charged on both wings.

Enemy resistance quickly collapsed. Ruthven's first line broke with little fighting. The reserve, behind the hedges, at first attempted a stand, but when their mounted officers made off the troops joined the flight.

Sir Bevil Grenville wrote an exultant account of the action to his wife:

> My dear love,
> It hath pleased God to give us a happy victory this past Thursday being the 19th of January, for which pray join me in giving God [thanks]. We advanced yesterday from Bodmin to find the enemy, which we heard was abroad; or, if we miss finding him in the field, we were resolved to unhouse him in Liskeard or leave our bodies in the highway. We were not above three miles from Bodmin when we had view of two troops of their horse to whom we sent some of ours which chased them out of the field, while our foot marched after our horse. But night coming on we could march no further than Boconnoc Park where (upon my Lord Mohun's kind motion) we quartered all our army that night by good fires under the hedge.
>
> The next morning (being this day) we marched forth at about noon, came in full view of the enemy's whole army, upon a fair heath between Boconnoc and Braddock Church. They were in horse much stronger than we, but in foot we were superior as I think.
>
> They were possessed of a pretty rising ground which was in the way towards Liskeard, and we planted ourselves on such another against them within musket shot, and we saluted each other with bullets about two hours or more, each side being willing to keep their ground of advantage, and to have the other come over to his prejudice. But after so long delay, they standing still firm and being obstinate to hold their advantage, Sir Ralph Hopton resolved to march over to them and to leave all to the mercy of God and valour of our side.
>
> I had the van; and so, solemn prayers in the head of every division, I led my part away. Who followed me with so good courage, both down the one hill and up the other, that it struck a terror in them. Whilst the seconds came up gallantly after me, and the wings of horse charged on both sides.
>
> But their courage so failed them as they stood not our first charge of foot but fled in great disorder and we chased them divers miles. Many were not slain because of their quick disordering, but we have taken about six hundred prisoners. Amongst which Sir Shilston Carmedy is one, and more are still brought in by the soldiers; much arms they have lost, eight colours we have won, and four pieces of Ordnance from them.
>
> And without rest we marched to Liskeard and took it without delay, all their men flying from it before we came.
>
> And so I hope we are now again in the way to settle the country in peace . . . Let my sister and my cousins of Clovelly, with your other friends, understand of God's mercy to us. And we lost not a man . . .

The Parliamentarian rout was apparently hastened when the townsmen of Liskeard attacked their rear. Hopton suggested that the Cornish deliberately spared many of the fugitives, possibly because some of them were their pre-war neighbours, but the final tally of prisoners was at least 1,250 men, with perhaps 200 dead. Two Parliamentarian demi-cannon and a number of smaller pieces were captured, probably abandoned in the lanes leading to Liskeard.

As the victorious Royalists occupied Liskeard that night, Ruthven fled to Saltash, which he garrisoned before decamping to Plymouth. Pressing his pursuit, Hopton stormed Saltash on 22 January, taking 140 prisoners. Meanwhile a second Parliamentarian force under Lord Stamford had begun an advance on Launceston, but, on learning of the rout at Braddock Down, it retreated to Plymouth. Cornwall was for the moment clear of the enemy and the initiative was back in Hopton's hands.

Shifting Fortunes

The Royalists followed up their advantage by again invading Devon, and advancing as far as Tavistock, before turning their attention to Plymouth. The town's defenders had expected an imminent attack after Braddock Down and had hastily strengthened their defences. Possibly because of the need to build up their forces, both sides entered into abortive negotiations for a truce. These never had any realistic prospects of success, for the Royalists demanded free passage for their forces to join the King, whilst all garrisons in Devon and Cornwall were to be either dismantled or handed over to Royalist control.

Another factor influencing Hopton was that, without the support of the Cornish Trained Bands, who continued to refuse to cross the Tamar, he could not establish a full blockade of Plymouth — which was, in any case, unlikely to fall as long as it could be supplied by sea. As in his previous attempt, Hopton could do no more than establish a series of outposts on the approaches to Plymouth, an endeavour which Bevil Grenville, for one, felt was unlikely to succeed. Writing to his wife on 20 February, he remarked that 'Plymouth is still supplied with men and all sorts of provisions by sea which we cannot hinder, and therefore for my part I see no hope of taking it.'

His forebodings were justified the next day. The Royalists had stationed two regiments at Modbury to secure the eastern flank of their blockading troops. Meanwhile the Parliamentarians had been struggling, with some difficulty, to organise a relieving force in Devon. Eventually soldiers were mustered in the north of the county, and, advancing south-westwards, they chased a small Royalist detachment under Sir John Berkeley out of Chagford. Berkeley fell back to join Hopton's main force, leaving the way clear for the Parliamentarian troops to move into south Devon and link up with men from Plymouth.

Early on 21 February they attacked Modbury, the Royalists crediting them with 9–10,000 men, a figure certainly inflated for a force which included many ill-armed 'clubmen'. The Royalist defending force was formed around John Trevanion and William Godolphin's Regiments of Foot, with some dragoons and about five light guns. In all there were perhaps 1,500–1,700 Royalists in the town. They threw up barricades covering the entrances to Modbury and placed musketeers in the hedges on its approaches, but after an exchange lasting for about three hours, with light casualties, the Royalist outposts were forced back into Modbury.

As the Parliamentarian assault continued into the night, the Royalists ran short of ammunition. Fighting eventually died down around midnight, and in the early hours of the morning the Royalists slipped away through an unguarded exit, leaving behind five guns. The defenders probably lost about a hundred men, compared

A large variety of guns were employed during the war. They ranged from heavy whole and demi-cannon used in siege operations through to a variety of light, basically anti-personnel guns such as that shown at the bottom of this contemporary illustration.

with an admitted dozen casualties for the Parliamentarians. Losses had been relatively light because most of the fighting had taken place in the cover of thick hedgerows and steep banks, men firing more or less blindly in the direction of the enemy. The Royalist prisoners had a narrow escape from a more unpleasant fate, however, as the Earl of Stamford, it was reported, briefly considered giving them to the Barbary corsairs in exchange for existing captives who might be enlisted in the Parliamentarian forces. He was dissuaded on the grounds of likely Royalist reprisals.

The reverse at Modbury caused Hopton once again to abandon his attack on Plymouth. He pulled back to Tavistock. The Parliamentarians, for their part, were unable to follow up their success because of large-scale desertions among their troops, 'the undisciplined forces of this county . . . consisting chiefly of Trained Bands altogether incapable to follow our victory into Cornwall . . .'

All that had been achieved at the end of the campaign was an uneasy stalemate, with both sides in need of a breathing space to rebuild their forces. A truce was agreed in March, and this would eventually be extended until 22 April; under it, the Royalists pulled back once more to the west of the Tamar. Neither side had any interest in a permanent peace settlement in the area, which would in any case have been rejected by their national leaderships, but they saw the truce as a much-needed opportunity to rest and strengthen their forces in preparation for what they hoped would be a decisive campaign.

The Earl of Stamford was able to raise three new regiments of foot, giving him a total of about 3,500 — 2,000 of them seamen — and eight troops of horse. He also imported 1,500 muskets from the Low Countries. For their part, the Royalists brought in at least one shipload of munitions from France, and on 10 April the Royalist gentry and freeholders of Cornwall agreed to a weekly assessment of £750 on Cornwall and a voluntary loan of £3,000 in plate.

By 22 April both Royalists and Parliamentarians had been mobilised for the next round. The main Parliamentarian field force of about 1,500 foot and 200 horse, under the energetic twenty-five-year-old Major General James Chudleigh — Stamford was at Exeter, incapacitated by gout — was mustered at Liston, three miles from the Cornish border. The Royalists were numerically superior, but disadvantaged in having to spread their forces to guard the several crossing places of the Tamar. Their main force, consisting of the 1,200 men of Grenville's Regiment, accompanied by Hopton, was at Launceston. Chudleigh decided to make Launceston his initial objective, and during the evening of 22 April his advance guard moved up to the eastern end of Polson Bridge, awaiting the expiration of the truce. Early on Sunday, 23 April, the Parliamentarians seized the bridge and advanced into Cornwall.

Hopton, informed by his scouts of the enemy's anticipated advance, led half of Grenville's Regiment out to occupy a strong defensive position on Beacon Hill, to the east of Launceston, whilst sending messages for the remainder of his army to join him with all possible speed. William Godolphin's Regiment soon began to arrive, whilst Grenville's men had taken up position in the hedges at the foot of Beacon Hill, with reserves of pikes and musketeers higher up its slopes.

Chudleigh's men advanced across the fields towards the Royalist positions and commenced a largely ineffective fire, the soldiers as usual firing blindly from cover. As the morning wore on, Hopton was reinforced by Lord Mohun's Foot Regiment and some horse under Sir John Berkeley. The Parliamentarians were now significantly outnumbered but meanwhile had made slight progress, forcing the Royalists' front line back towards their reserves.

Fighting is unlikely to have been continuous, and at about 5 p.m. Hopton was joined by Slanning's and Trevanion's Regiments. He was at last strong enough to counter-attack, and in the early evening he mounted a three-pronged offensive, under himself, Berkeley and Francis Bassett, employing 3,000 foot and 600 horse. His flanks threatened, Chudleigh began to fall back, but he was rescued from a potentially serious situation by the arrival from Plymouth of about 600 men of Sir John Merrick's grey-coated foot regiment, who launched a counter-attack. This helped ease enemy pressure sufficiently for Chudleigh's army to fall back across Polson Bridge to its starting point at Liston.

The Parliamentarians admitted to the loss of seven to ten dead and forty wounded, whilst the Royalists' losses are unlikely to have been much heavier. Hopton's pursuit was half-hearted, partly because a hut containing the enemy powder magazine blew up, injuring a number of his men, and also because of a mutiny among the Cornish. As Hopton later wrote, scathingly, 'The common soldiers, according to their usual custom after a fight, grew disorderly and mutinous, and the commanders were always short of means either to satisfy them or otherwise to command them.' By the time any serious follow-up could be organised, Chudleigh had withdrawn to

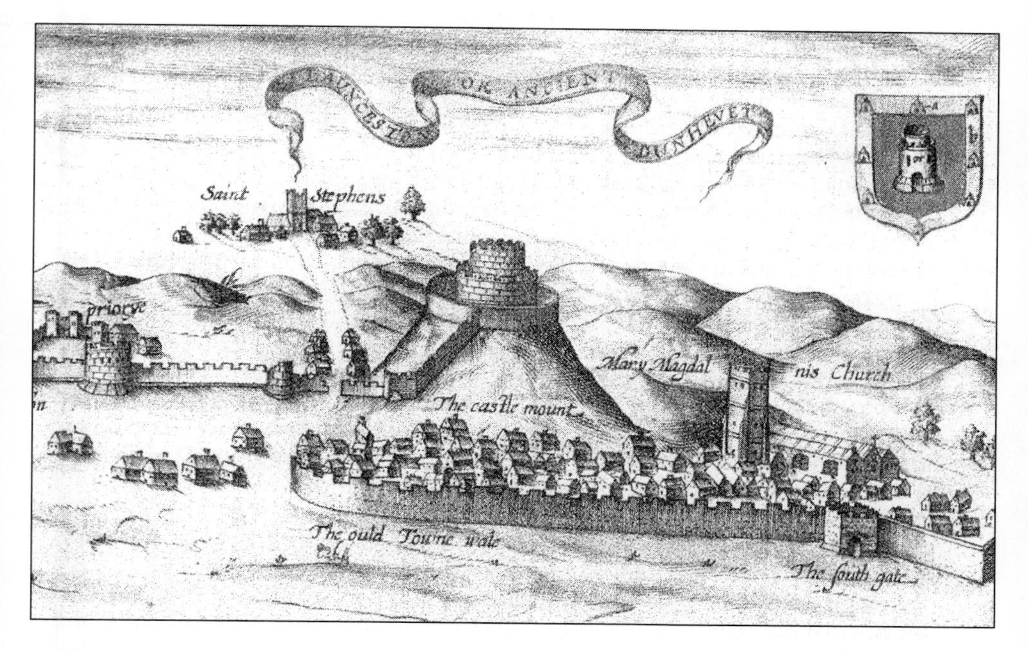

Launceston was an important administrative centre, as well being strategically located near one of the crossings of the River Tamar. The castle, shown here in John Speed's map (c. 1612), was evidently in a state of disrepair by the time of the Civil War.

Okehampton. Here a number of his units went their separate ways, leaving him with about 1,000 foot and three or four troops of horse.

Hearing that the Parliamentarians at Okehampton were in a state of some confusion and disagreement, and with low morale, the Royalist commanders decided to exploit the situation with a dawn attack on 25 April. As the Royalist army formed up for a night march across Sourton Down towards Okehampton, they seemed to a complacent Hopton to be 'the handsomest body of men that had been gotten together in those parts all that war'. Crossing Sourton Down, the Royalists formed into column. They were led by 150 mounted dragoons, intended to act as scouts, followed by 150 horse. Then came half of the foot, led by Mohun's Regiment, followed by the artillery, in advance of the remainder of the foot, with another 300 horse and dragoons bringing up the rear.

Eventually news of the enemy's approach reached an astounded and furious Chudleigh. As he wrote later,

> By the intolerable neglect of our lying deputy Scout Master, we were surprised by the whole enemy body of horse and foot . . . and by the incomparable dullness of Sergeant-Major Price, the carriage of our Ammunition and artillery was dismissed, contrary to orders express against it, so that I was forced to this sad Dilemma, to loose the Ordnance, and all that we had here(which in

all probability would have been the ruin of the whole Kingdom) or to hazard a desperate Charge (which for ought I knew might have routed the whole Army).

Chudleigh, however, a veteran of the Irish wars and a combative character, determined not to give up without a fight. After a hasty council of war he led three troops of horse, totalling 108 men, out on to Sourton Down. Breaking his force down into six squadrons, each of eighteen men, Chudleigh deployed them across the down in ambush, with a hill behind them which helped them blend into the darkness.

By now the Royalist column was approaching, blissfully unaware of the imminent threat, 'never, as they conceived, in better order, nor in better equipage, nor ever, (which had like to have spoiled all) in less apprehension of the Enemy.' Hopton, with Sir John Berkeley and Colonel Thomas Bassett, was riding at the head of the column, the commanders, by Hopton's own later admission, 'carelessly entertaining themselves', when suddenly the first of Chudleigh's troops, under Captain Thomas Drake, came galloping out of the darkness, firing at Hopton's dragoons and yelling, 'Fall on, fall on, they run, they run!'

The result was chaos. The Royalist dragoons, for the most part raw levies, broke and fled, carrying away with them in their rout the 150 cavalry immediately behind them, together with Sir Ralph Hopton and his companions. The remainder of the Parliamentarian cavalry now joined in the attack. Early in the fighting they overheard the Royalist field word, 'Launceston', which enabled them to add to the confusion.

The first body of Cornish foot were already alarmed and demoralised by the sudden onset of a thunderstorm, and the attack by the enemy horse, the small number of whom was not apparent in the darkness, proved too much. The Cornish fled in all directions, 'the night growing tempestuous with Hideous Claps of Thunder', and the lightning reportedly igniting the powder charges of some unfortunate musketeers. With cries that 'the militia fought not against them but the Devil', a large number of Hopton's foot disappeared into the night, throwing away their weapons and equipment to hasten their flight.

Surging on, Chudleigh's men briefly overran the Royalist guns and wagons, but the impetus of their attack was faltering. Hopton's artillery guard counter-attacked, retaking their guns and positioning them behind a ditch. Here they were reinforced by musketeers from Slanning's Regiment, some of whom had sharpened stakes — known as 'Swedish or swines' feathers' — which could be erected as a defence against horse.

Avoiding these organised opponents, the Parliamentarian cavalry spent some time skirmishing with parties of fleeing Royalists. In the meantime Chudleigh ordered his foot in Okehampton to advance and attack Slanning's position. However, the lighted match of the Parliamentarian musketeers was sighted glowing in the darkness by the Royalists, who discharged two drakes at them. The Parliamentarian foot broke in their turn and made off.

There was little more that Chudleigh could do to exploit his success and his troopers, having hung lighted match in gorse bushes to deceive the enemy, withdrew. By now the storm and heavy rain had reached a new intensity, and the Royalists pulled back to Launceston.

Sourton Down had been a major humiliation for Hopton. Considerably more of his men had been routed and scattered than killed or captured, though he lost a large quantity of weapons and other equipment. He probably suffered between 20 and 100 dead and a dozen prisoners. Of the latter,

> Captain Wrey being then but 15 years of age, and little stature, but a spritely [*sic*] gallant youth, and then commanded a company in the Lord Mohun's Regiment that had the vanguard was taken prisoner and carried down to Okehampton, but the troopers that took him being careless of him and thinking him but a trooper's boy he took the opportunity to make his escape into the night, and three days after[wards] returned into Cornwall with a dozen or 13 Musketeers of the stragglers that he had collected.

It was a small comfort in a thoroughly humiliating and exasperating episode for Hopton, and one for which he had only himself to blame.

The Royalists spent the next few days at Launceston, reorganising and rounding up stragglers. They then advanced again to Tavistock, and considered another move against Okehampton. However, hearing that the Parliamentarians there had been reinforced, Hopton again fell back across the Tamar.

Stratton

Among the most valuable prizes taken by the Parliamentarians was Hopton's correspondence, including a letter from the King's Secretary of State ordering Sir Ralph to march into Somerset in order to link up with Royalist forces from Oxford

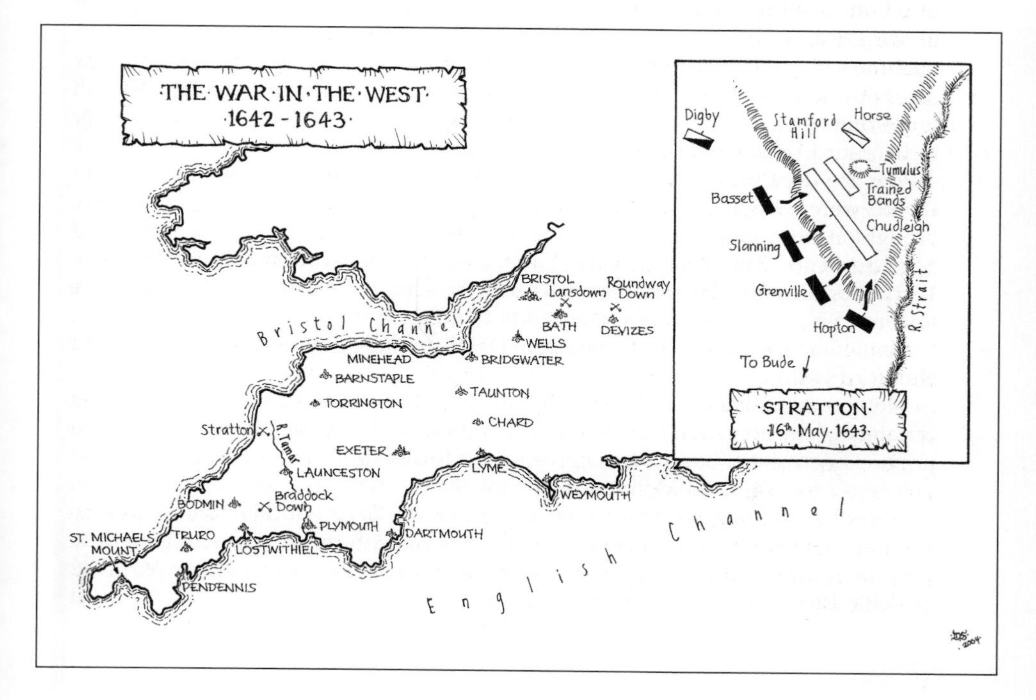

The Tree Inn, Stratton, traditionally held to have been Hopton's headquarters before the battle, and possibly the scene of his Council of War held the previous night.

under the command of the Marquis of Hertford, still the King's Lieutenant General in the West, and Prince Maurice. Delighted by this insight into enemy plans, Stamford, still at Exeter, forgot his gout and 'leapt out of [his] chair for joy'. He saw an opportunity both to frustrate Hopton's strategy and at last to conquer Cornwall for Parliament.

Stamford spared no effort in raising the largest possible field army for what he saw as the deciding contest of the war for the West. Parliamentarian garrisons in Devon were stripped of every man who could be spared, and more troops were brought in from Somerset. By these means Stamford was able to muster an army of 1,400 horse and 5,400 foot, of which he assumed personal command. Advancing to Torrington in north Devon, Stamford then crossed the Cornish border, heading towards Sir Bevil Grenville's heartlands around Stratton. Here, on 14 May, the Parliamentarians occupied a steep-sided, flat-topped ridge which is now called Stamford Hill.

Hopton meanwhile had been taking his own steps to meet the threat. With no certainty of the point at which Stamford would make his attack, the Royalists, as on previous occasions, had had to spread their forces to cover as many threatened points as possible. Lord Mohun's Regiment, 900 strong, was stationed at Liskeard; Sir Nicholas Slanning, with 1,000 men, was at Saltash; 700 men under John Trevanion were at Launceston; and Sir Bevil Grenville, still with the strongest regiment of 1,200 men, was in the vicinity of Stratton. In an effort to raise more troops, on 12 May the Royalist Commissioners of Array met at Bodmin and ordered the third man out of every hundred in the militia to be levied for active service, whilst Sir Francis Bassett made feverish efforts to raise additional funds.

On the same day that the Commissioners met at Bodmin, Hopton, at Launceston, learnt of Stamford's advance towards north-east Cornwall, and set off northwards to meet him, gathering in his troops as he went. The Royalists reached the village of North Pethervin that night and camped on the common outside. They had had little time to gather supplies, and both officers and men had to content themselves with a dry biscuit apiece. The next day, after morning prayers, the Royalists marched on towards Stratton.

On their way they had a brief skirmish with some Parliamentarian horse and dragoons. These may have been from the force of 1,200 commanded by Sir George Chudleigh that Stamford had just detached with orders to attack Bodmin and break up Royalist attempts to muster the *posse comitatus* there. Their departure left Stamford with about 200 horse and something over 5,000 foot. The latter included Sir John Northcote's 1,200-strong Devon Regiment and Merrick's 700 greycoats who had saved the day for the Parliamentarians in the action at Launceston. Added to these were various smaller units and some of the Devon Trained Bands.

The skirmishing with Chudleigh's departing cavalry had slowed Hopton's march so that he only reached the village of Week St Mary, about five miles north of Stratton, that night. Once again dining frugally on a biscuit each, the Royalists stayed on the alert in the darkness in case of enemy attack. Stamford, however, had no intention of quitting the strong position which he held. The steep-sloped hill was protected on its southern side by a number of small,hedged fields at its foot, whilst the eastern

Many of the lanes in the vicinity of the battlefield are evidence of the gradient up which the Royalist advance took place.

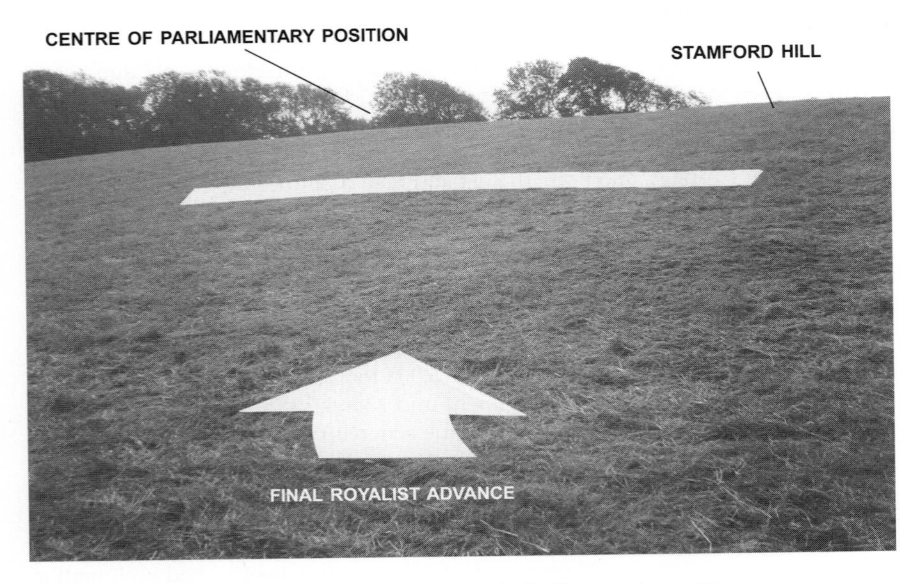

The crest of Stamford Hill, which formed the centre of the Parliamentarian position.

side was too steep to be easily assailable,and was shielded by the River Neet running at its foot. The defenders had the further advantage of an ancient earthwork at the summit. The various possible crossing points of the Neet were defended by parties of Parliamentarian musketeers, but towards nightfall the Royalists drove off one outpost near Efford House and crossed the river, the other Parliamentarian pickets falling back on their main position.

That night the Royalist commanders held a Council of War. They had few choices open to them. They would have to attack Stamford's strong position the next day, before Sir George Chudleigh's horse could return.

Skirmishing between parties of musketeers in the hedgerows began soon after dawn. Soon afterwards all of the Royalist army had crossed to the east bank of the Neet and were deployed in five bodies. Four of these were of foot, each about 600 strong, a mixture of pikemen and musketeers and each accompanied by two light guns. The fifth division was formed by 500 horse and dragoons under Sir John Digby who were held back to the west to guard against Chudleigh's horse.

Contrary to some accounts of the battle, based on Clarendon's partly inaccurate version of events, the Royalists did not attack on all four sides of the hill. Their first column, led by Hopton and Lord Mohun, was to advance on the south side of Stamford Hill. The second division, led by Grenville and Sir John Berkeley, would advance to their left along a lane. The third division, formed from Slanning's and Trevanion's Regiments, was to attack on the left of Grenville, whilst the final body, under Sir Thomas Bassett, now Major General of Hopton's foot, and William Godolphin were to the left of them. The Royalists' right flank was thus covered by

A view north-westwards from the Parliamentarian positionS on Stamford Hill. The hedgerow in the centre background marks the approximate start line of the Royalist assault.

the River Neet whilst their left lay towards the coast, partly protected by Digby's horse.

By now the Cornish foot were probably armed according to the recommended 2:1 musket/ pike ratio. The pikes were deployed where possible in narrow, deep columns in the lanes themselves, with bodies of 200 musketeers initially stationed on each flank, though these rapidly deployed forward to engage in a firefight in the hedges with their Parliamentarian opposite numbers. The main Parliamentarian force, occupying the slope of Stamford Hill, was probably deployed in two lines. The first consisted of Stamford's more reliable troops — Northcote's and Merrick's men — with the more uncertain Trained Bands forming a second line to their rear. Their whole front probably extended for about 900 yards.

Stamford's men were well supplied with ammunition and provisions, and their commander's aim was to hold the Royalists until Chudleigh's cavalry returned and then finish them off. Stamford's main fear was that, if the Royalists were able to work their way round on his right, they could then attack Stamford Hill on its less formidable northern side.

Action probably began in this direction on the north-western face of the hill, with skirmishing between opposing parties of musketeers, at around 5 a.m. It was some time later that more intense fighting began as the four Royalist infantry columns tried to force their way uphill under fire from the enemy musketeers in the hedges. There was little or no hand-to-hand fighting at this stage and the pike advance seems to have stalled whilst the musketeers, with unrecorded pauses, continued to

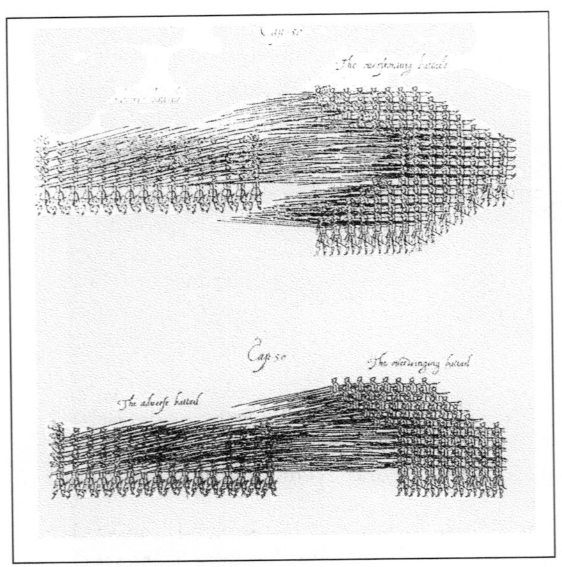

'Push of pike'. Engagements between opposing pikemen might range from ineffectual 'fencing' at pike-length through to a shoving match resembling a rugby scrum, aimed at disordering the opposing force and pushing them back. Most casualties were suffered in the pursuit, though a pikeman who, like Grenville, lost his footing might be trampled in the press.

exchange fire until after 3 p.m. By then the Royalists were down to their last four barrels of powder, an unpleasant situation which the commanders decided to conceal from their men. A hasty Council of War ordered a synchronised assault by all four columns, with orders not to fire until they reached the summit.

Although the musketeers must have been fairly tired by now, the pikemen, who had not so far been seriously engaged, would still have been quite fresh, and their advance made good progress. The main threat to the Parliamentarians appeared to be from Grenville's column, including men of his own Regiment, generally speaking the best of the Cornish foot. Major General James Chudleigh, probably without orders from Stamford, counter-attacked the Royalist column leading his own pikes. Grenville was at the head of his pikes whilst Sir John Berkeley was with one of the flanking bodies of musketeers. Grenville was knocked down in the initial scrimmage of 'push of pike' between the opposing forces and suffered severe bruising, but then Berkeley and his men took the Parliamentarians in flank, no doubt employing their musket butts, and forced them back in confusion.

Chudleigh was captured, and his abortive counter-attack had probably cost the Parliamentarians some of their most seasoned troops. Confusion began to spread through Stamford's ranks and the Royalist advance quickened, their columns converging as they neared the summit of the hill. Shortly before 4 p.m. the Royalist commanders met just to the south of the highest point and 'they embraced with unspeakable joy, each congratulating the others services, and did acknowledge the wonderful blessing of God.' The united Royalist force then turned left towards the summit, the Parliamentarians beginning to crumple under their attack. In a Parliamentarian version of events:

The fight continued twelve hours, in all which time our poor Gray-coats and Volunteers did their parts, very manfully; but our base cow-hearted Trained Soldiers, as soon as they came to do service ran all away, and Brought the whole Army into an utter Confusion.

With its weaker brethren in flight, the whole of Stamford's army collapsed. There was an inclination to blame the débâcle on Chudleigh's counter-attack:

. . . the Van of a brave Army killed, taken and routed with him. After all this the Earl had 3,000 men left, store of Ammunition and Ordnance, which himself stood to, and intreated them to stand also, but no intreaty could persuade above thirty of them to stay.

The Parliamentarian army had been comprehensively routed. Stamford himself, with Colonel John Weare, fired a last defiant salvo from their artillery before riding off for the safety of Bideford. The Royalists were too tired to mount any prolonged pursuit but they had done enough. Their prizes included, among many other arms and supplies, thirteen guns, one mortar and seventy barrels of powder. They probably lost about ninety dead, compared with a Parliamentarian total of about 300 killed and 700 prisoners. Among the latter was James Chudleigh, who shortly afterwards changed sides.

The Parliamentarian cavalry under Sir George Chudleigh — who would soon follow his son's example and defect — had successfully carried out their mission at Bodmin, but when news of the disaster at Stratton triggered an uprising the town they had to fight their way out to reach Plymouth and eventually pull back into Somerset.

The Royalist commanders knew that their victory had at last secured Cornwall for the king's cause. Sir Francis Bassett wrote joyfully and incoherently to his wife:

Dearest Soul, Oh, Dear Soul, praise God everlastingly. Read the enclosed: Ring out your Bells, Raise Bonfires, publish the Joyful Tidings, Believe these Truths. Excuse me writing larger. I have not time. We march on to meet our Victorious Friends, and to seize all the Rebels left, if we can find any such living.

Chapter II

Lansdown and Roundway Down, 1643

After their crushing defeat at Stratton there was no prospect of the Parliamentarians in Devon mounting any opposition outside the walls of their garrisons. Morale in the Cornish Royalist army had reached its highest point in the war. James Chudleigh, writing from the Royalist camp to his father, announced his decision to change sides, telling him, 'I never saw any army freer from vice, nor more religiously inclined than I perceive the whole genius of this Army to be.'

Some, with good grounds, might have thought this image of the Cornish soldier as paragon to be idealised. The Cornish were as eager for loot as any others, and always ready to mutiny, even against their own officers, but Hopton, with his alleged motto 'Pay well, and hang well', and because of his victory at Stratton, had won their confidence in a way that no other outsider ever achieved.

Stamford retreated to Exeter, and Hopton made his way back to Launceston to find Sir George Chudleigh and the Parliamentarian horse gone. Here he was brought news that Hertford and Maurice had left Oxford around 14 May, bound for the West, and received the King's orders to march to join them.

It was a striking tribute to Hopton's hold over his Cornish troops that they apparently made no serious murmur about the prospect of marching far from their native county. The Royalist forces crossed the Tamar on Whit Sunday (21 May) heading first for Okehampton, where they were joined by Sir Bevil Grenville's Regiment from Stratton. Approaching Exeter, Hopton once again summoned the town to surrender but on its expected defiance wasted no time in attempting to take it. Leaving two companies of foot and one of dragoons at Columb St John, three miles to the east of Exeter, in order to contain the garrison, the Royalists continued their eastward march and on 4 June linked up with Hertford and Prince Maurice at Chard.

The independent existence of the Cornish Army was at an end, and this union with the wider Royalist world inevitably led to changes. The most immediate was a step down in authority by the Cornish Army commanders, though the resulting command structure was hardly more clear-cut than previously. Hertford was General. His role was, however, fairly limited, partly through his personal inclinations and limitations but also because of the forceful personality of his Lieutenant General, and second-in-command, Prince Maurice. Hopton and his officers had to be slotted into this new arrangement, and Sir Ralph, as 'Field Marshal General', became effectively third in command of the united forces. Hopton did not complain of this arrangement in his memoirs, but he deplored the effects which joining the forces from Oxford had on the discipline of his own troops. He was described by his friend, Clarendon, as 'a man superior to any temptation, and abhorred enough the licence and levities with which he saw too many corrupted.' Nevertheless, while he had partially succeeded in keeping his Cornish troops in check, he found the situation very different among the Oxford horse: 'there began the disorder of the horse visibly to break in upon the prosperity of the public proceedings. . . . the Generals were never able to repress the extravagant disorder of the horse to the ruin and discomposure of all.'

It is only fair to add the comments about the Cornish made by Captain Richard Atkyns of Prince Maurice's Regiment of Horse:

> . . . the Cornish foot could not well brook our horse(especially when we were drawn up upon corn) but they would many times let fly at us: these were the

Prince Maurice (1621-52)

Younger brother of Prince Rupert, Maurice was described by Clarendon as understanding 'little more of the war than to fight very stoutly when there was occasion.' This was probably a criticism of Maurice's political awareness rather than his military skills. A wild youth, Maurice began his military career at an early age, attending the Siege of Breda in 1637.In 1642 he accompanied Rupert to England to offer his services to his uncle, the King, and saw action at Powick Bridge and Edgehill. In independent command, he met Waller in the Severn Valley and defeated him at Ripple Field before moving to the West as Lieutenant General of Horse to Hertford.

A prickly and somewhat uncultivated character, Maurice readily offended civilians and those of delicate sensibilities. Overshadowed even during his lifetime by his brother, he was nevertheless a capable cavalry commander, more at ease among his soldiers than at Court.

very best foot I ever saw, for marching and fighting; but so mutinous withal, that nothing but but an alarm could keep them from falling foul of their officers.

Atkyns confirms Hopton's view of the mutinous nature of the Cornish infantry, but it is at least possible that some of the animosity resulted from the natural jealousy felt by the foot soldier towards the advantages held by a horseman when it came to obtaining loot. Atkyns says as much when he recounts an incident which occurred shortly after the armies joined: '[While] observing a hole in an elder hedge, I put in my hand and took out a bag of money; which if our foot had espied (who were also upon the search) they had certainly deprived me of both it and life.'

For the moment, however, animosities were diminished by action. Parliamentarian forces in Somerset were in some disarray — no match for the united Royalist army. The Parliamentarian troops initially in Somerset consisted of about 1,000 Somerset and Devon horse, William Strode's 400-strong regiment of foot and about 2,000 of the Somerset Trained Bands. Also on his way was Sir William Waller, the Parliamentarian commander who had recently made a name for himself with a string of victories along the Welsh border. He was, however, held up for a week in Gloucester, trying to obtain pay for his troops, and did not reach Bristol until 6 June. Even when he arrived in Bath two days later, he would spend the next three weeks organising his forces.

In the meantime there was little to oppose the advance of the combined Royalist army of 2,300 horse and dragoons, 4,000 foot (three-quarters of them Cornish) and 16 guns. Hertford's first objective was the strategically important town of Taunton. When the Royalists arrived before the town on 5 June, its authorities opened surrender negotiations but were pre-empted by a pro-Royalist uprising which forced the Parliamentarian troops in Taunton to retreat. Many of them were captured, along with a considerable quantity of arms and ammunition, and this probably signalled the effective disintegration of most of the Somerset Trained Band forces. Part of the garrison of Bridgwater, also probably Trained Bands, mutinied as well, and within two days all resistance to the Royalists in Western Somerset had collapsed.

The Royalist army rested at Taunton for two days, and when their advance was resumed Hertford, probably to the relief of his officers, remained behind for a time to organise the administration of the area. Prince Maurice was now in effective command, assisted by Hopton, whose local knowledge would have been invaluable. The remaining Somerset Parliament-

Richard Atkyns (1615–77). After raising a troop of horse early in 1643 and serving throughout the Western campaign of that year, Atkyns left the Army after the capture of Bristol believing the war virtually won. He died in debt in Marshalsea Prison, London.

Sir William Waller (1598-1668)
Waller fought alongside Hopton for the Protestant cause in Bohemia in 1618. Later, as an MP, he was a moderate supporter of the Parliamentarian opposition to King Charles and became one of its commanders on the outbreak of Civil War. In 1642 he captured Portsmouth, and won a string of minor victories in the south which won him popular acclamation and the nickname 'William the Conqueror'. He gained further success on the Welsh Border in the spring of 1643, but was defeated by Prince Maurice at Ripple Field. He was a competent soldier, noted for his swift marches and skilful use of terrain.

arian forces — about 2,000 mainly horse and dragoons under Sir Alexander Popham — were around Glastonbury and Wells, whilst Waller, with a similar number of men and eleven guns, had just arrived at Bath.

Chewton Mendip
On 11 June the main Royalist force advanced to Somerton, having sent a detachment, including Colonel Joseph Bampfield's Regiment of Foot from Hertford's force, to strengthen the blockade of Exeter. Maurice's initial aim was to occupy Glastonbury and Wells and push out Popham's forces, who were reported to be preparing to unite with Waller. As the Royalists advanced deliberately towards Glastonbury, the Parliamentarians slowly withdrew before them. Skirmishes between the advancing Royalists and the Parliamentarian rearguard continued throughout 12 June. The Parliamentarians made a more serious stand between Glastonbury and Wells, where musketeers concealed in the hedges beside the road held up Maurice's men for over an hour. There was further brief resistance in Wells, as Parliamentarian horse covered the retreat of their foot, making their way up into the Mendip Hills overlooking the town. At the summit the Parliamentarian cavalry deployed on open ground to protect their foot and wagons, which were entering the village of Chewton Mendip.

The Royalist foot quartered for the night in Wells whilst Maurice and the horse continued to harass the retreating enemy. In the evening a cavalry action developed about a mile outside Chewton Mendip. The main Parliamentarian force was now in the village, with a rearguard of foot halted outside, on the edge of open ground and with horse drawn up about a mile in front of them.

The Royalist pursuit was headed by the young Earl of Carnarvon, a typically dashing Cavalier, who immediately charged the enemy without waiting for reinforcements. He met with initial success, routing his opponents, chasing them through the village and taking guns, ammunition and wagons, but, as was often the case in such situations, he lost control of his men, who kept up the pursuit to within five miles of Bath. Here they encountered some of Waller's horse, possibly including

Sir Arthur Haselrigg's redoubtable cuirassier regiment — the 'Lobsters' — and were chased back through Chewton Mendip.

News of the reverse was carried to Maurice's men, who had begun to settle down for the night but had now hastily to reassemble and move up to support Carnarvon. Maurice, advised by Sir John Berkeley to pull back through Chewton and deploy on the open ground outside the village, where he would not be encumbered by the narrow lane, was joined by some of Carnarvon's rallied men, although the Prince had only part of his own regiment with him. Waller's horse halted when they sighted Maurice and his troopers, and deployed. They consisted of a regiment of horse in two divisions, each of about 250 men, with dragoons in the hedges on their flanks and more dragoons a few hundred yards in front. Maurice launched an attack that ran into trouble when a sudden mist descended (a common Mendips phenomena), and confusion broke out. The Parliamentarian dragoons, uncertain where the enemy were, opened an ill-aimed fire and then mounted up and rode off. Maurice routed one division of Parliamentarian horse but was then taken in the rear by the other. The Prince was wounded in the head and captured, though not identified.

Richard Atkyns takes up the story:

> . . . we were then a mile on our way towards our quarters, when Colonel Brutus Buck acquainted our regiment with this unwelcome news; which I heard first, having the honour to command the rear division of the regiment. My Lieutenant-Colonel [Guy Molesworth], my Major [Thomas Sheldon] and the rest of the officers, advised what to do in this case; and the result was, that Prince Maurice himself having commanded his regiment to their quarters, they were subject to a council of war, if they should disobey command; to which I answered [being senior captain] that I was but a young soldier, and if they would give me leave, I would draw off my division and run the hazard of a Council of War; they told me, they might as well go themselves, as give me leave to go; but if I would adventure, they would not oppose it, but defend me the best they could.
>
> I drew off my division with all possible speed, and put them in order, which were not above 100 men; and before we had marched twelve score yards, we met the Lord Carnarvon's regiment scattered, and running so terribly, that I could hardly keep them from disordering my men (though in a large champaign) at last I met his Lordship with his horse wellnigh spent, who told me I was the happiest sight he ever saw in his life: I told him I was no less glad to see his Lordship; for as yet I had no command for what I had done, and now I hoped he would give me command publicly, to preserve me from the censures of a Council, which he did. The enemy seeing a party make towards them left their pursuit, and drew up at Chewton, and the Lord Carnarvon, the Lord Arundell of Wardour, with myself, marched in the head of my party; this was about half an hour before sunset; and when we came within 20 score [yards] of the enemy, we found about 200 dragoons half musket shot before a regiment of horse of theirs in two divisions, both in order to receive us. At this punctilio of time, from as clear a sunshine day as could be seen, there fell a sudden mist, that we could not see ten yards off, but we still marched on; the

Robert Dormer, Earl of Carnarvon (d.1643). A dedicated Royalist, Carnarvon fought in the Second Scots War and at Edgehill. He was killed at the First Battle of Newbury (20 September 1643).

dragoons amazed with the mist, and hearing our horse come on; gave us a volley of shot out of distance, and disordered not one man of us, and before we came up to them, they took horse and away they run, and the mist immediately vanished. We had then the less work to do, but still we had enough; for there were 6 troops of horse in 2 divisions, and about three or four hundred dragoons more, that had lined the hedges on both sides of their horse; when we came within 6 score of them, we mended our pace, and fell into their left division, routing and killing several of them.

The dragoons on both sides, seeing us so mixed with their men that they could not fire at us, but they might kill their own men as well as ours; took horse and away they run also. In this charge, I gave one Captain [Edward] Kitley quarter twice, and at last he was killed: the Lord Arundell of Wardour also, took a dragoon's colours, as if it were hereditary to the family so to do; but all of us overran the Prince, being prisoner in that party: for he was on foot, and had a hurt upon his head, and I suppose not known to be the Prince. My groom coming after us, espied the Prince, and all being in confusion, he alighted from his horse, and gave him to the Prince, which carried him off: and though this was very great success, yet we were in as great danger as ever: for now we were in disorder and had spent our shot; and had not time to charge [load] again; and my Lieutenant [Thomas Sandys] and Cornet [Richard Holmes] with above half the Party, followed the chase of those that ran, within half a mile of their army; that when I came to rally, I found I had not 30 men; we had then three fresh troops to charge, which were in our rear; but by reason of their marching through a wainshard [wagon yard] before they could be put in order: I told those of my party, that if we did not put a good face upon it and charge them presently, before they were in order, we were all dead men or prisoners; which they apprehending, we charged them; and they made as it were a lane for us, being as willing to be gone as we ourselves. In this charge there was but one of my troop killed and 8 hurt. For the wounded men of my troop, and also of my division I received 20 s [20 shillings] a man of Sir Robert Long, then Treasurer of the Army, which was all the money I ever received for myself, or troops, during the war.

The weary Atkyns found what quarters for the night he could in Wells, not knowing the fate of some of his officers and men, though he discovered next morning

Harquebusiers (from John Cruso, Military Instructions for the Cavalerie, *1635). The standard cavalrymen of the Civil War, the troopers depicted are well equipped ith a pot helmet, back and breast plates, a sword, a pair of pistols and a carbine. In reality, however, not all cavalry were so lavishly provided for.*

that only two of them, including Lieutenant Sandys, had been captured. Atkyns also

> . . . waited upon Prince Maurice, and presented him with a case of pistols, which my uncle Sandys brought newly out of France; the neatest that I ever saw, which he then wanted; but as yet he knew not the man that mounted him, nor whose horse it was: when I saw the horse I knew him, and the man that rid him that day; which was the groom aforesaid: the Prince told me he would not part with the horse, till he saw the man that horsed him, if he were alive, and commanded me to send him to him; which I did that day, and when he came to the Prince, he knew him, and gave him 10 broad pieces, and told him withal, that he should have any preferment he was capable of.

However 'the graceless fellow' deserted soon afterwards. Atkyns returned, doubtless hungry, to his quarters, 'where there was a handsome case of a house, but totally plundered, and neither bread nor beer in it; but only part of a cheddar cheese, which, looking blue, I found my foot-boy giving to my greyhounds, and reproving him for it; he cried, saying there was nothing else to give them.'

The action at Chewton Mendip had cost the Royalists about thirty to forty men, the Parliamentarians rather more.

Lansdown

A fortnight's lull followed. The Royalists remained in the vicinity of Wells and Waller stayed around Bath. Both armies needed to reorganise and build up their strength in preparation for the next round of the contest.

Waller was reasonably strong in horse; after he had merged his own and the Western Brigade he had in the region of 2,500 troopers, but he was much less well off in terms of foot. On 22 June Sir William and his Lieutenant General, Sir Arthur Haselrigg, wrote to the Speaker of the House of Commons, warning him that

> ... we as your servants cannot but acquaint you with our condition. We have a body of horse by God's blessing able to do the Kingdom good service. The enemy lies still at Wells. That part of the country is altogether unfit for horse. It grieves our souls we dare not attempt what we desire. We must not hazard your trust like fools, neither can we stay here and starve. We have long and often supplicated you for money. Find us but a way to live without it, or else we humbly beg a present supply, if not this horse will certainly disband, which makes our hearts to bleed.

Shortly afterwards eight troops of Haselrigg's 'Lobsters' arrived from London, escorting a consignment of money, which, Waller acknowledged, 'came very seasonably to keep life in us when we were in a grasping condition.'

He remained, however, critically short of foot, and those he had were in a poor condition. Popham's Regiment had been mauled in the fighting near Wells, whilst those of William Strode and Thomas Essex were weak and the battered remnants of

John Speed's Plan of Bath (c.1611)

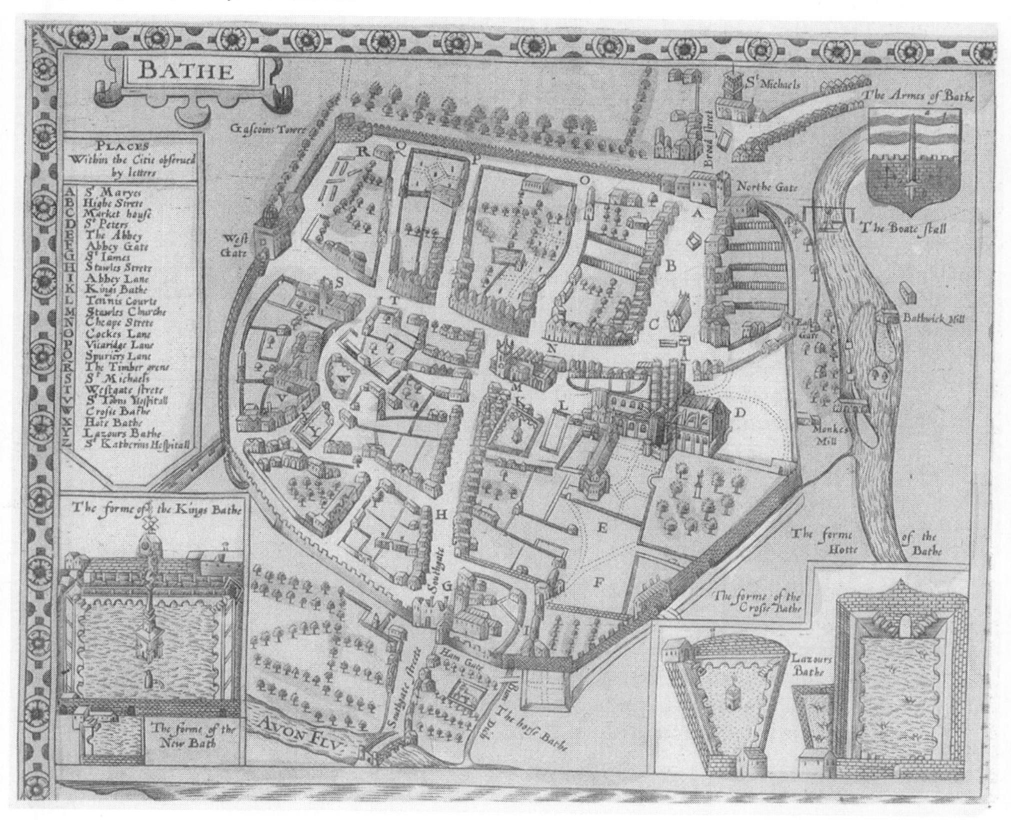

the Earl of Stamford's men unimpressive. Waller asked for reinforcements from Bristol, but the city's Governor, Nathaniel Fiennes, was reluctant to weaken his garrison. Waller wrote frantically:

> Good Sir, Sure you think we have both a lame and patient enemy, that will . . . stay till we be ready to answer his return. . . . What good will this regiment do Bristol if we perish? Let not the west of England be lost for a little monies, neither send your supplies too late. There is a time which wise men will not let slip.

However, by early July Waller still only had about 1,500 foot.

During this lull in activity Sir Ralph Hopton wrote to his old comrade-in-arms of the Continental Wars, Sir William Waller, evidently suggesting a meeting. He may only have intended a social encounter, but Waller replied in one of the most moving letters of the war:

> Sir,
> The experience I have had of your Worth, and the happiness I have enjoyed in your friendship are wounding considerations when I look at this present distance between us. Certainly my affections to you are so unchangeable, that hostility itself cannot violate my friendship to your person; but I must be true to the cause wherein I serve; The old limitation usque ad aras [even to the altar, i.e., for ever] holds still, and where my conscience is interested, till other obligations are swallowed up. I should most gladly wait on you according to your desires but that I look upon you as engaged in that party, beyond a possibility of retreat and consequently incapable of being wrought upon by any persuasion. And I know the conference could never be so close between us, but that it would take wind and receive a construction to my dishonour; That great God, which is the searcher of my heart, knows with what a sad sense I go upon this service, and with what a perfect hatred I detest this war without an Enemy, but I look upon it as Opus Dominini [God's work] which is enough to silence all passion in me. The God of peace in his good time send us peace, in the meantime fit us to receive it. We are both upon the stage and must do those parts that are assigned us in this tragedy. Let us do it in a way of honour, and without personal animosities, whatsoever the issue may be, I shall never willingly relinquish the title of
>
> your most affectionated [*sic*] friend and faithful servant,
> William Waller
> Bath 16 June 1643

On 19 June the Royalist Council of War had decided to make defeating Waller their priority and to follow him 'whichsoever way he went'. At the end of June they resumed active operations, advancing from Wells to Frome. Further skirmishing ensued. The Parliamentarians scored a minor success when a force of 250 of their cavalry commanded by Major Francis Duett beat up the quarters of Sir James Hamilton's Regiment of Horse at Leigh on Mendip, taking fifteen officers, 97 men, 140 horses and 60 cases of pistols.

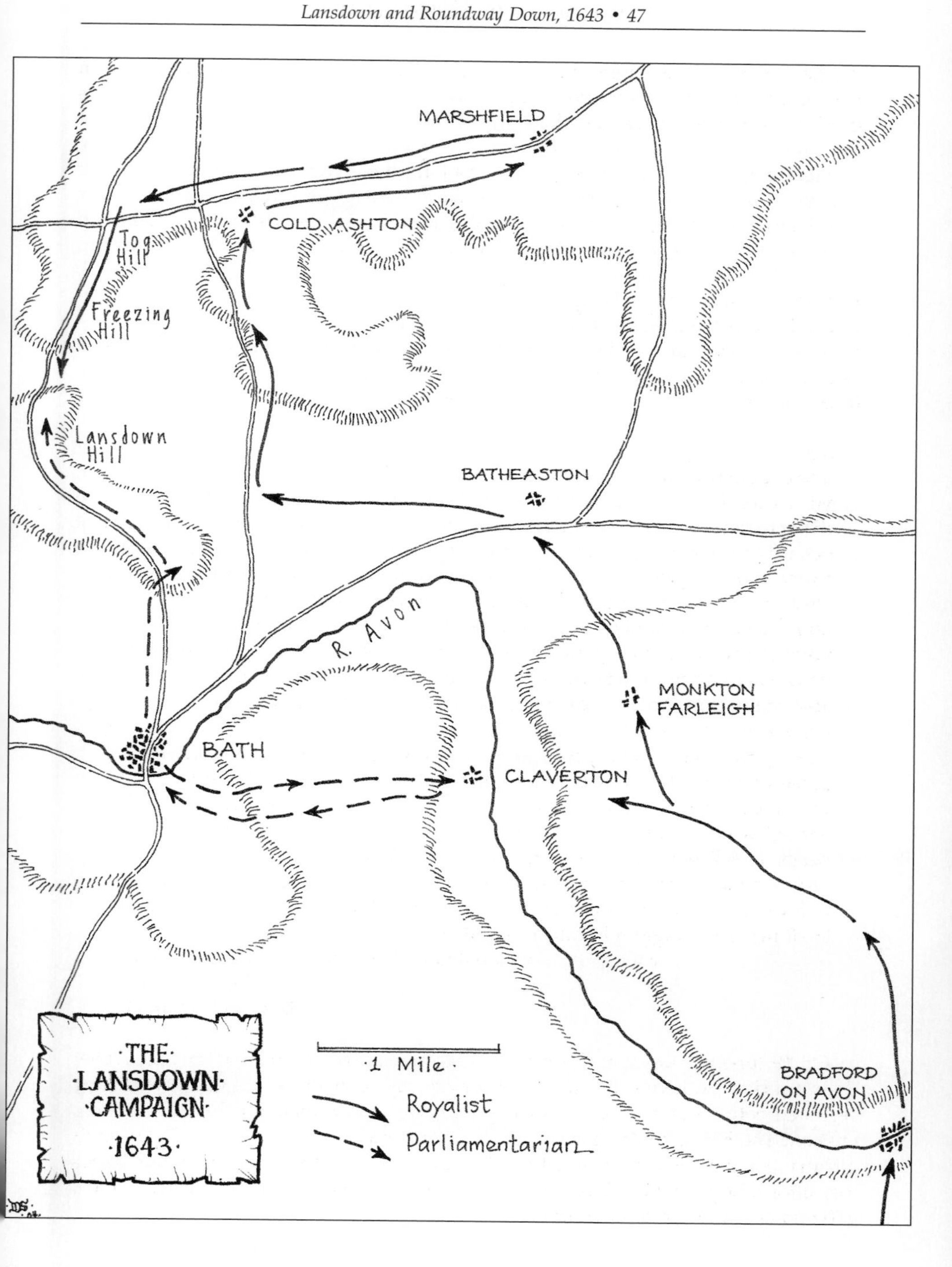
MARSHFIELD
COLD ASHTON
Tog Hill
Freezing Hill
Lansdown Hill
BATHEASTON
R. Avon
MONKTON FARLEIGH
BATH
CLAVERTON
BRADFORD ON AVON
·THE·
·LANSDOWN·
·CAMPAIGN·
·1643·
·1 Mile·
Royalist
Parliamentarian

On 2 July the Royalists seized the bridge at Bradford-on-Avon, eight miles from Bath. Bath itself was protected on its southern side by the River Avon, so the Royalists moved northwards to launch their attack from that direction. Waller had at last been reinforced by Alexander Popham's Regiment of Foot from Bristol, and drew up his forces on Claverton Down, overlooking the Avon. In a countermove that evening, Waller sent a force under Colonel Robert Burghill across the river near Claverton by means of a temporary bridge. The Parliamentarians occupied Monkton Farleigh Hill, their infantry concealed in neighbouring woods. Next morning skirmishing began, during which the Cornish foot forced their opponents back towards the Avon, taking two light guns. As darkness fell Maurice sent the Cornishmen across the river towards Waller's main position.

The wily Parliamentarian commander was not to be drawn, however, for, as Colonel Walter Slingsby, commanding Lord Mohun's Regiment of Foot, observed, 'thus had the shifty Rebel deluded us one day with a party, hoping to make us weary with dancing about him, or else to fight where he pleases.'

The commanding 225-foot height of Lansdown Hill, five miles to the north-east of Bath, remained unoccupied, and a hastily summoned Royalist Council of War, consisting of Hopton, Carnarvon, Mohun and Slanning, met that night to decide whether to take possession of it. By now, with darkness almost on them, the Royalist forces were widely scattered by the day's operations, with only one body of horse and foot immediately available. The Royalist officers felt that it would be unwise to try to hold Lansdown with so small a force but sent a message to Hertford, urging him to occupy it as soon as possible with his entire strength.

However, as the Royalists approached early on 4 July they discovered that Waller had got there before them. Sir William had too good an eye for terrain to have missed the importance of holding Lansdown Hill if he were to retain Bath, and, as

Lansdown Hill as seen from the north by the approaching Royalists. The trees partly hide the steepness of the ascent.

This panoramic view from the summit of Lansdown Hill, with the Cotswolds on the horizon, demonstrates the advantages for an army positioned on the hill.

Slingsby acknowledged, 'Indeed the General of the Rebels was the best shifter and chooser of ground when he was not master of the field that I ever saw, which are great abilities in a soldier.' The discomfited Royalists spent several hours eyeing Waller's position, before, at about 1 p.m., falling back on the village of Marshfield. About 1,000 musketeers lined the lanes, covering the Royalist withdrawal and beating off a probing attack by a Parliamentarian forlorn hope.

Next morning Waller pushed his forces forward, taking up a position at the eastern end of Lansdown, on a cross-ridge known at its western end as Hungry Hill. Here the Parliamentarians began constructing a breastworks of stones, reinforced by timber cut from nearby woods. Advancing again from Marshfield, the Royalists deployed on the 700-foot Tog Hill, about one and a half miles from the Parliamentarians.

Throughout the next few hours skirmishing continued in the hedgerows and in the valley separating Lansdown from the next ridge a mile to the north-east, Freezing Hill. Spasmodic fighting continued for four or five hours before Parliamentarian musketeers, supported by Captain John Butler's troop of Haselrigg's 'Lobsters', forced the Royalists back to a large cornfield at the foot of Tog Hill.

Seeing no prospects of driving Waller from his strong defensive position, the Royalist commanders ordered a withdrawal back to Marshfield, but as the movement began Waller unleashed his own attack, made by Major Duett with 200 horse, supported by 200 dragoons under a Scottish professional soldier, Colonel Carr. Maurice sent the Earl of Carnarvon and his horse to counter-charge, whilst Sir Nicholas Slanning with 300 musketeers engaged Carr's dragoons in the lanes near Freezing Hill.

The Royalist horse were roughly handled by their opponents, particularly after Waller sent Burghill's Regiment of Horse to support Duett's horse by falling on Carnarvon's flank. Confused fighting took place in the valley between Freezing Hill

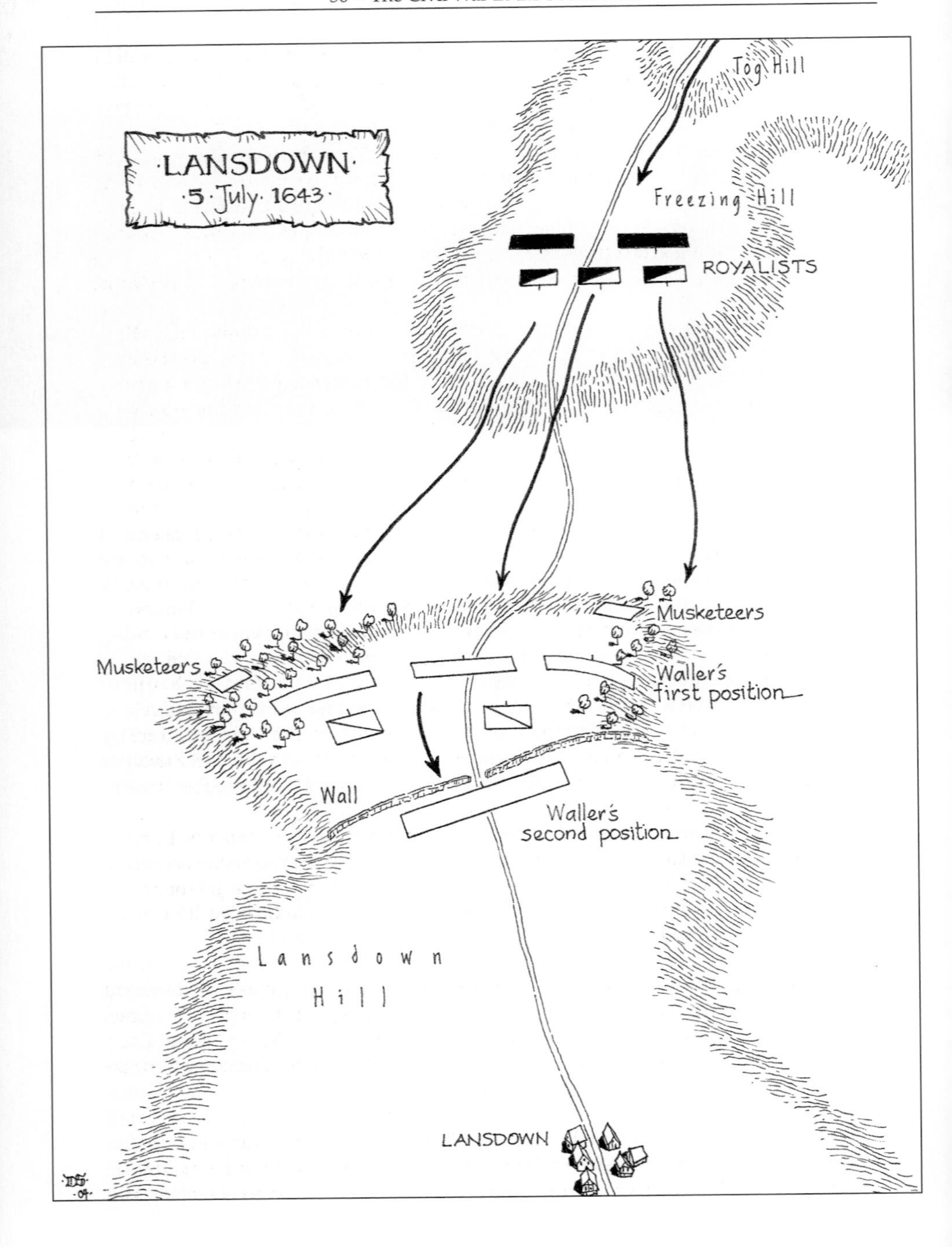
LANSDOWN
5 July 1643
Tog Hill
Freezing Hill
ROYALISTS
Musketeers
Musketeers
Waller's first position
Wall
Waller's second position
Lansdown Hill
LANSDOWN

and Lansdown, during which the Royalists reoccupied the large cornfield, 'which we got with much difficulty and hazard, our horse receiving some dangerous foils; so that had not our foot been excellent we had certainly suffered there.' The advancing Cornish musketeers forced the Parliamentarian dragoons out of 'the walls and hedges at the far end of the field', and with both Burghill and Carnarvon slightly wounded in the action the Parliamentarians began to withdraw to their main position. Their horse suffered some disorder in the narrow lane leading up to Lansdown as they came under fire from the Royalist musketeers in the hedges, but they had the satisfaction of having retaken two light guns lost in the fighting on 2 July.

Richard Atkyns, who was closely involved, gives a vivid account of the action:

> . . . our horse being placed before our foot and cannon, were commanded off troop by troop; and being within half musket shot of the hedges lined on both sides by their dragoons; several horses were killed, and some of our men; their muskets playing very hard upon our horse, made us retreat so disorderly, that they fell foul upon our foot; and indeed there was not room enough for us to retreat in order, unless we had gone upon the very mouths of their muskets: I suppose the stratagem was to draw on their party of horse upon our foot and cannon, the better to rout them, and then our horse to fall in upon them to do execution; for the dragoons making their way by pioneers, were not discovered till they shot. Our commanders seeing the army in such disorder, and the enemies' horse marching near us; commanded the then Marquis Hertford's Lifeguard of horse to charge them, who never charged before; which was then commanded by that honourable and loyal person the Lord Arundel of Trerice; I seeing all like to have been lost, unless a sudden check were given to this party of horse; desired him to give me leave to charge with him, with these words: 'that we would answer for one another that day': we charged together, and both of us fell upon the commander-in-chief [Burghill] and hurt him so, that he reeled and wheeled off, and the party with him: there were several others hurt and killed on each side, of the Marquis's Lifeguard Mr Lee and Mr Barker, gentlemen of quality.
>
> Twas now time to draw out a party of commanded men, but the Lord Carnarvon (according to his usual course) drew up his regiment as soon as possible, and pursued them almost to their body, and took several prisoners; in which charge (or soon after) he had a shot in the leg, that disabled him for further service at that time.

It was now late in the afternoon, and Waller remained firmly ensconced behind his defences on the crest of Lansdown. According to one Royalist version of events, 'The enemy to encourage us to prosecute this success, gave all the symptoms of a flying army, as blowing up of powder, horse and foot running distractedly upon the edge of the hill, for we could see no further.'

Richard Atkyns, however, sent with a party of horse to reconnoitre, reported that the enemy were still in position. As well as his main barricaded line, Waller had also placed parties of horse and musketeers in the thick woods on his flanks, whilst the steep slope to his front, up which a narrow, walled lane ascended, would

The head of the lane by which Grenville and his pikes reached the summit of the hill.

be a formidable proposition for an attacker. Slingsby commented grimly that 'thus fortified stood the fox gazing at us.'

What exactly happened next is unclear. Slingsby remarked that the Cornish foot called out to be allowed to 'fetch those cannon', and a Royalist advance began. It is far from certain who authorised it. There was apparently no preliminary Council of War, and it may have been a unilateral action commenced by the Cornish, born of their recollection of a similar successful assault at Stratton. Hopton was probably present, but his account makes no reference to consultations with his fellow senior officers.

The plateau at the summit of Lansdown Hill, where the main action between Grenville's foot and Waller's horse took place.

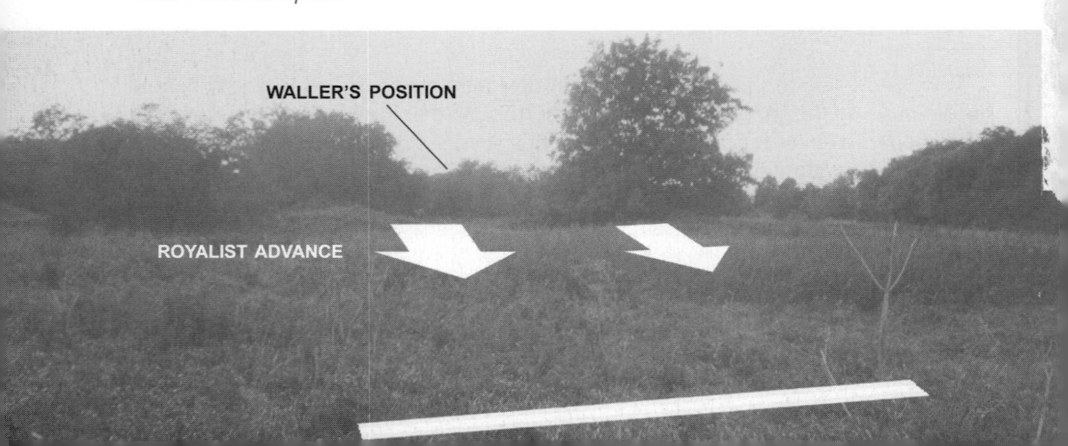

Authorised or not, the assault was to cost the Royalists dearly. The attack was made by Sir Bevil Grenville and the Cornish pikemen advancing in column in the centre up the lane, with musketeers to their left in the fields and woods and cavalry on the right.

For much of their ascent, the Royalist pikemen in the centre were protected by dead ground, or by the banks, hedges and walls along the winding lane. Even so, the Royalists came under artillery and eventually musket fire. Slanning, probably still leading his musketeers, had his horse shot under him and the cavalry suffered severely, failing to give much support to their foot.

Waller pulled his men back from the immediate crest of the hill, allegedly to provide more space for his own cavalry to counter-attack. As Grenville's column of pikes breasted the hill, they came under a storm of case shot and musket fire which brought them to a halt. Haselrigg's 'Lobsters' now launched at least three counter-charges against the hedgehog of Cornish pikes. In the third of them Grenville was mortally wounded by a blow to the head with a pole-axe, whilst his captain lieutenant fell dead clutching a captured enemy colour. Many of the 'Lobsters', including Haselrigg, suffered wounds to poorly protected legs and thighs, whilst losses were heavy among their horses. Waller himself led several more charges, including two by his own regiment.

By now the Cornish musketeers and a few of the horse were coming up to the support of the pike hedgehog. Atkyns was among the arrivals:

> As I went up the hill, which was very steep and hollow, I met several dead and wounded officers brought off; besides several running away, that I had much ado to get up by them. When I came to the top of the hill I saw Sir Bevil Grenville's stand of pikes, which certainly preserved our army from a total rout, with the loss of his most precious life: they stood as upon the eaves of a house for steepness, but as unmoveable as a rock; on which side of this stand of pikes our horse were, I could not discover; for the air was so darkened by the smoke of the powder, that for a quarter of an hour together (I dare say) there was no light seen, but what the fire of the volleys of shot gave, and 'twas the greatest storm that ever I saw, in which though I knew not whither to go,

Traces of a 'hollow way' on the northern edge of the battlefield at Freezing Hill. This was probably one of the routes by which Royalist troops — in this case horse — reached the summit.

> nor what to do, my horse had two or three musket bullets in him presently, which made him tremble under me at that rate, and I could hardly with spurs keep him from lying down; but he did me the service to carry me off to a led horse, and then died: by that time I came up the hill again, the heat of the battle was over, and the sun set, but still pelting at one another half musket shot off: the enemy had a huge advantage of ground upon our men, for their foot were in a large sheep-cot, which had a stone wall about it as good a defence against any thing but cannon as could be, and ours upon the edge of the hill, so steep that they could hardly draw up; 'tis true there were shelves near the place like Romish [Roman] works, where we quartered that night, but so shallow that my horse had a bullet in his neck: we pelted at one another till half an hour before day, and then we heard not any noise, but saw light matches upon the wall, which our commanders observing, sent one to discover whether they had quit the field or not, who brought news that they were gone.

Waller's men were positioned behind a stone wall, about 400 yards back from the crest, through which they made gaps for their artillery to fire and for parties of horse to mount attacks. The Royalist musketeers had by this time taken up position 'amongst the many little pits betwixt the wall and the wood from whence we galled them cruelly . . . Thus stood the two armies taking break looking upon each other, our cannon on both sides playing without ceasing until it was dark, legs and arms flying apace.' At nightfall the Royalist position remained critical as they maintained a precarious foothold on the crest of the hill:

> About 11 of the clock we received a very great volley of shot but not mixed with cannon, by which some of us judged that he [Waller] was retreating and gave this at his expiring. But the general apprehension through our army was that the enemy had intention to try to push in the night for their ground, which they had so dishonourably lost; for we were then seated like a heavy stone upon the very brow of the hill, which with one lusty charge might well have been rolled to the bottom.

At nightfall the Royalists had called a hasty Council of War, attended by Prince Maurice, Hopton, Sir James Hamilton and Major Sheldon. The situation seemed grim: over half of the cavalry, henceforward scornfully termed by the Cornish foot as 'runaway horse', had scattered, some fleeing as far as Oxford. The Cornish infantry had suffered heavy losses, including perhaps 200 dead and 300 badly wounded, compared with admitted Parliamentarian losses of just over twenty men. The decision of the commanders was: 'if the enemy fall upon us, every man to shift for himself.'

For much of the night that possibility seemed uncomfortably real. The Royalists stood to arms, but after about 1 a.m. all enemy firing ceased, though lighted match could be seen glimmering in the enemy lines. After about an hour Hopton sent a man creeping forward to Waller's position. He returned to report the enemy gone, with only burning match left fixed to pikes wedged in the wall.

There are a number of stone walls of indeterminate date on the southern edge of the battlefield. This one, to the south of the Grenville monument, is probably part of the second position held by Waller.

Waller had decided to withdraw to Bath, 'our horse being in continued service for three days together, and without meat or water for the space of at least twenty-four hours, and our foot much tired.' He also knew, following the losses suffered by the Royalists, that 'we could easily recover the hill again, and so fall upon the enemy, to prosecute the victory next morning.' This might have been a case of being wise after the event, though Walter Slingsby admitted that 'we were glad they were gone, for if they had not, I know who had within an hour.'

Both sides claimed Lansdown as a victory, Waller with rather more justification, for although the Royalists had taken about 400 arms and ten barrels of powder they

The hollows in this area of uneven scrub-covered ground to the south of the plateau are probably the remains of the 'pits' in which Royalist musketeers took cover in the later stages of the battle.

The rectory at Cold Ashton where Sir Bevil Grenville died.

were no nearer to capturing Bath, or to defeating Waller, and had suffered horrific casualties, not least Sir Bevil Grenville, who died soon after being carried to Marshfield. Moreover, events next morning — 6 July — were to worsen the Royalist position further.

The March to Devizes

Their failure to defeat Waller at Lansdown had left the Royalists in serious difficulties. Quite apart from the casualties they had suffered, their expenditure of ammunition had left them in no condition to fight another major engagement. Waller's army was still intact, and so long as it remained in the field the Royalists had no chance of taking their principal objective in the area, the port of Bristol.

As the Western Army prepared once again to withdraw to Marshfield, Hopton and some of his officers were surveying the scene of the previous day's fighting. Atkyns saw what happened next:

> [Hopton] was then viewing the prisoners taken, some of which was [*sic*] carried upon a cart wherein was our ammunition; and (as I heard) had match to light their tobacco: I had no sooner turned my horse, and was gone 3 horses' lengths from him, but the ammunition was blown up, and the prisoners in the cart with it; together with the Lord Hopton, Major Sheldon, and Cornet Washnage, who was near the cart on horseback, and several others: it made a very great noise, and darkened the air for a time, and the hurt men made lamentable screeches. As soon as the air was clear, I went to see what the matter was: there I found his Lordship miserably burnt, his horse singed like parched

> leather, and Thomas Sheldon complaining that the fire was got within his breeches, which I tore off as soon as I could, and from as long a flaxen head of hair as ever I saw, in the twinkling of an eye his head was like a blackamoor . . . Sir Ralph Hopton was a miserable spectacle, his head swollen as big as two heads and his eyes near burnt out.

The Royalists, in a state of considerable despondency, spent the night at Marshfield. It seemed that their only remaining chance lay in marching on towards Oxford in the hope of receiving reinforcements from there and so, early on 7 July, they set off in the direction of Chippenham, Hopton, still half-blinded, being carried in the Marquis of Hertford's coach.

It is not clear if Waller yet knew of the misfortune which had befallen his old friend. He remained at Bath for two days in order to rest his men and receive a consignment of 60 barrels of powder from Bristol. On learning that the Royalists were heading in the direction of Devizes, Waller resolved to pursue them, 'not doubting but his [Hopton's] bulk of plunder would something retard his journey.' During the evening of Friday 7 July the Parliamentarians set out from Bath on the trail of their opponents. In the Royalist Army morale had slumped. Already stricken by the loss of Sir Bevil Grenville, the Cornish soldiers 'drooped for their Lord [Hopton] whom they loved.'

Waller, meanwhile, arriving at Marshfield, had made an appeal for support to the local country people. Although this probably did not bring in many recruits, he received plentiful intelligence concerning enemy movements and was soon close on the Royalists' heels. By 4 p.m. on 8 July Waller's scouts were within three miles of Hertford's army, then at Chippenham. For a time, as both armies deployed, it seemed as if a battle might begin at once, but only minor skirmishing took place that day.

Next morning, taking advantage of an exchange of prisoners, Hertford sent to Waller the rather strange proposal that 'there might be good quarter betwixt our Armies, and that we might fight no more in holes, but in the champion.' Waller, doubtless with tongue in cheek, responded that he would 'meet his Lordship that afternoon about Sherston in the Plain: and if his lordship wanted powder . . . he would lend him some for the fight.'

As Sherston was about eight miles to the north, Sir William cannot have expected his proposition to be taken seriously, and, at about noon on the 9 July, the Royalists resumed their march to Devizes. Pressing their pursuit, Waller's vanguard of horse scattered some Royalist cavalry still in Chippenham. As they rode on beyond the town, on what may well have been a hot afternoon, many stragglers at the roadside surrendered.

About three miles from Devizes the Parliamentarian horse caught up with the Royalist rearguard. In the first shock of the attack the Royalist horse broke, though Prince Maurice rallied them and, according to Richard Atkyns,

> Lieutenant-Colonel Richard Neville [Carnarvon's Regiment] was commanded to bring up the rear, which he did with that gallantry, and good conduct, that we killed as many of the enemy as they did of us, and when the foot came

> safe to the Vies [Devizes] and that the Horse only had done that service; instead of calling us runaway horse (which the Cornish used to do) they called us gallant horse; for the Cornish foot knew not till then the service of horse.

Atkyns perhaps exaggerates the role of the cavalry, for a key part in holding off the Parliamentarians was played by Lord Mohun's Regiment of Foot, commanded by Lieutenant-Colonel Walter Slingsby. Ordered by Prince Maurice to hold a ford over a stream just north of the village of Rowde Hamlet, Slingsby and his men stood their ground for thirty minutes, at the cost of forty men, but gave the army enough time to reach the safety of Devizes.

The Royalists' difficulties were far from over. It was too dark for Waller to launch an assault that day, but Hertford and his commanders had few grounds for optimism. As night fell Waller sent three troops of horse to secure the high ground of Roundway Down, on the north side of Devizes, and next morning concentrated his whole army there. Some Royalist horse made a brief sortie from Devizes to investigate but withdrew before making contact. Devizes was defended on its northern side by the town ditches and the remains of its medieval defences and protected by steep slopes to the south and west. Some spasmodic attempts had been made at the start of the war to improvise some additional fortifications, and the Royalists continued work on these as well as barricading the roads leading into the town.

However, the Royalist Council of War which met on the night of 10 July around Hopton's bedside faced a grim prospect. There were only two barrels of powder remaining and supplies of match for the musketeers was critically short. Hopton was able to deal with the latter problem by ordering his General of the Ordinance to requisition all the bed cord in the town. Boiled in resin, this provided over 1,500 pounds of match, enough for immediate needs. Other ammunition remained short, and a supply convoy from Oxford escorted by the Earl of Crawford's small brigade of horse had been captured by the Parliamentarians.

There was insufficient fodder in the town for the horses, and it was resolved that Hertford, Maurice and the cavalry should break out at midnight and head for Oxford to seek help. Richard Atkyns described their perilous escape:

Defences could take many forms. Those at Devizes were partly improvised, and the streets may have been blocked by barricades, including the type of spiked, moveble 'turnpikes' shown here.

> About midnight, our horse marched, or rather made an escape out of town, leaving the foot behind us; we met not the enemy at all, but some of our own forces, whose fears scattered them, and we were like to fall foul upon each other: they were part of the horse that should have come to our assistance, but hearing ill news secured themselves, viz, the Lord Crawford's regiment, between three and four hundred, and Colonel James Long's regiment, between two and three hundred. At the break of day, we were at least 8 miles from Devizes, and free from all enemies between that and Oxford; Prince Maurice and several of the officers galloped to Oxford, to be there as soon as they could; but my horse had cast two shoes, and I was forced to stay behind to set them at Lambourn, where leaning against a post, I was so sleepy that I fell down like a log of wood, and could not be awakened for half an hour: 'twas impossible then to overtake them; so I went to Faringdon, being not able to reach Oxford that night; I fell off my horse twice upon the downs, before I came to Faringdon, where I reeled upon my horse so extremely that the people of the town took me to be dead drunk: when I came to my house (for there I sometimes lived) I despatched a man and horse presently to the Prince to receive orders, and desired my wife's aunt to provide a bed for me presently, where I slept at least fourteen hours together without waking.

Meanwhile, back in Devizes, Hopton and the foot were preparing to meet Waller's attack. There had been some skirmishing and a desultory artillery bombardment during the previous day, and on the morning of 11 July Waller began by sending Hopton a summons to surrender, telling him of the dispersal of Crawford's convoy and offering reasonable terms. It has been suggested that Sir William, knowing that his old friend lay wounded within the town, hesitated to attack, but it is far more likely that Waller hoped to avoid unnecessary losses among his own men. Hopton's response was to play for time: offering to open negotiations, he obtained a cessation of hostilities lasting until 6 p.m.

Waller admitted that, 'Being desirous, as he [Hopton] professed to prevent blood spilling we lost

Dragoons were essentially mounted infantry who rode into action and fought on foot. The soldier here is armed with a carbine. Note the swivel, allowing the gun to be quickly aimed and fired, by which it is secured to his belt.

Henry Wilmot, 1st Earl of Rochester (?1612–1658), was a professional soldier who served in the Netherlands and the Second Scots War. He was a competent second in command of the Oxford Army horse in 1642. Unfortunately, Wilmot's political naivety would lead to his downfall.

that day by not agreeing.' The only results were that arrangements were made for the passage of Sir Bevil Grenville's body through the Parliamentarian lines for burial and a valuable respite was thus gained for the Royalists. In the evening there was some renewed skirmishing between Parliamentarian musketeers and their Royalist counterparts in the hedgerows outside Devizes, but, once again, it was too late for Waller to mount a serious assault that day.

Next morning, 12 July, the Parliamentarian attack began in earnest. Waller had placed his guns on Coatefield, a hill near the town, and they opened fire. However, Slingsby explained that the Royalists had 'so barricaded the avenues, that their horse could not charge in upon us, neither durst their foot attempt us, we being almost twice their number, and better foot.'

The Parliamentarians managed to clear a few Royalist outposts but could get no further. Nevertheless, if only because he believed that his opponents would soon run out of ammunition, Waller was confident of speedy success. That night he wrote to the Speaker of the House of Commons: 'We hope God will not destroy this mighty army of the West. He has wrought wonders for us, and we hope the Lord will keep us from that great strength they expect from Oxford.'

Waller had sent to the Earl of Essex, asking him to intercept any relief force, and he remained confident that the next day would see the fall of Devizes, admitting later that 'so sure was I of victory that I wrote to Parliament to bid them be at rest, for that I would shortly send them an account of the numbers taken and the numbers slain.' Nevertheless, next morning, 13 July, Waller displayed no particular haste in renewing his assault and about noon his scouts brought news of the approach of a column of Royalist cavalry from the direction of Marlborough.

Roundway Down

Hertford and Maurice had arrived in Oxford during the morning of 11 July to find that King Charles and Prince Rupert, with many of their troops, had gone to meet Queen Henrietta Maria and her large convoy of munitions on their way from the north. The senior remaining officer in the Royalist capital was the Lieutenant General of Horse, Lord Wilmot. Recognising the importance of rescuing Hopton, Wilmot and Maurice, each apparently supposing himself to be senior, hastily threw together a scratch force of the cavalry remaining in Oxford and set off next day for the relief of Devizes.

After they had been joined at Marlborough by the survivors of the Earl of Crawford's brigade, recently mauled by Waller, the Royalist force consisted of three brig-

Waller's initial position.

ades of horse — Wilmot's, Sir John Byron's, and Crawford's — reinforced by some volunteers from Maurice's horse and totalling about 1,800-2,000 men in all. They also had two light guns. More importantly from Hopton's point of view, they brought with them a convoy of thirty-seven wagons containing ammunition for his foot.

Waller had sufficient warning to be able to deploy his own army to meet the threat. He deployed on Roundway Down, taking up a position on the slopes of the 795-foot high Roundway Hill. Facing him was a shallow bowl of ground, with Kings Play and Morgan's Hills on its northern rim. The Parliamentarian foot, about 1,800 men and supported by five guns, formed the centre of Waller's line, grouped into two divisions. The six regiments of horse, making a total of 2,000 troopers, were deployed on the wings, Haselrigg's brigade on the right and Waller's on the left. The Parliamentarians probably occupied a total frontage of about 1,000 yards. The Parliamentarian dragoons were left in the hedgerows around Devizes to guard against a Royalist sally.

It was probably at about 2 p.m. that the Royalists, still in column about two miles away on the top of Roughridge Hill, came in sight of Waller. Wilmot halted and

View from the Parliamentarians' position towards the Royalist start line on Roughridge Hill.

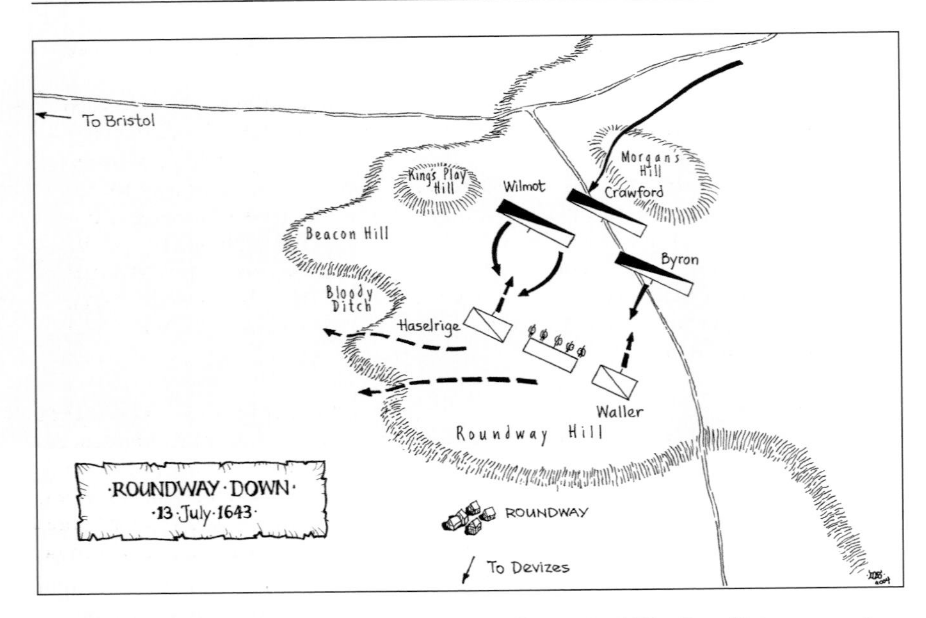

fired his two light guns as a signal to Hopton of his arrival. The Royalist commanders had undoubtedly hoped that the defenders of Devizes would sally in their support and take Waller in the rear, but although Hopton urged such a response at a hastily summoned Council of War his commanders, having previous experience of the wily Waller, suspected a trick and refused to move. Wilmot and Maurice were as a result alone, and a pause of about an hour followed whilst they considered their options. After consulting with the Earl of Carnarvon, whose previous experience of action against Waller would have been invaluable, Wilmot, who despite Prince Maurice's claims seems to have been effectively in command, decided to attack.

The Royalist brigades of horse, occupying a frontage of about 600 yards, were deployed in echelon on the south-western slopes of Morgan's Hill. Wilmot's own brigade, of about 800 men, was on the right, formed up in extended order and three ranks deep. To his left, and some distance behind, were the three regiments of the experienced cavalry commander Sir John Byron's brigade, also probably about 800 strong. Crawford's unsteady brigade was in reserve, probably with the wagons.

At about 3 p.m. fighting commenced when the opposing forlorn hopes of horse began skirmishing in the area between Roundway and Roughridge Hills. The Royalist force of about 300 men, commanded by Major Paul Smyth of Wilmot's Regiment, charged vigorously and drove their Parliamentarian opposite numbers back into Waller's left wing of horse, throwing it into temporary confusion. Seizing his moment, Wilmot ordered a general attack, taking Atkyns by surprise:

> . . . the charge was so sudden that I had hardly time to put on my arms, we advanced a full trot 3 deep, and kept in order; the enemy kept their station, and their right wing of horse being cuirassiers, were I'm sure five, if not six

deep, in so close order, that Punchinello himself, had he been there, could not have gotten in to them.

All the horse on the left hand of Prince Maurice his regiment, had none to charge; we charging the very uttermost man of their right wing: I cannot better compare the figure of both armies than to the map of the fight at sea, between the English and the Spanish Armadas, (only there was no half moon), for though they were above twice our numbers; they being six deep, in close order, and we but three deep, and open (by reason of our sudden charge) we were without them at both ends: the canoneers [*sic*] seeing our resolution, did not fire their cannon. No men ever charged better than ours did that day, especially the Oxford horse, for ours were tired and scattered, yet those that were there did their best.

Haselrigg had led his 'Lobsters' forward in support of his forlorn hope, hoping to punch through Wilmot's extended formation by weight of numbers, but found himself outflanked by the longer Royalist line. The Parliamentarians gave ground, then rallied, and briefly retook four guns which had been abandoned without firing a shot by their crews. However, with Byron now moving up in support of Wilmot, Haselrigg's men broke and fled towards Bath. Atkyns engaged a fugitive whom he believed to be Sir Arthur Haselrigg himself:

> . . . in six score yards I came up to him, and discharged the other pistol at him, and I'm sure I hit his head, for I touched it before I gave fire, and it amazed him at that present, but he was too well armed all over for a pistol bullet to do him any hurt, having a coat of mail over his arms and a head piece (I am confident) musket-proof, his sword had two edges and a ridge in the middle, and mine a good strong tuck. After I had slackened my pace a little, he was gone twenty yards from me. Riding three quarters speed and down the side of a hill, his posture was waving his sword on the right and left hand of his horse, not looking back whether he was pursued or not(as I conceive) to daunt any horse that should come up to him. After six score yards more I came up to him again . . . and stuck by him a good while, and tried him from head to saddle, and could not penetrate him, nor do him any hurt . . .

The area between the two armies in which initial skirmishing took place.

Haselrigg wounded Atkyns' horse with a sword thrust, and the Royalist responded in kind:

> . . . all this time we were together hand to fist.
>
> In this nick of time came up Mr Holmes to my assistance . . . and went up to him with great resolution, and felt him before he discharged his pistol, and though I saw him hit him, 'twas but a flea-biting to him; whilst he charged him, I employed myself in killing his horse, and ran him into several places, and upon the faltering of his horse his headpiece opened behind, and I had run him through the head if my horse had not stumbled at the same place; then came in Captain Buck, a gentleman of my troop, and discharged his pistol upon him also, but with the same success as before, and being a very strong man, and charging with a mighty hanger, stormed him and amazed him, but fell off again; by this time his horse began to be faint with bleeding, and fell off from his rate, at which said Sir Arthur, 'What good will it do you to kill a poor man?' said I 'take quarter then', with that he stopped his horse, and I came up to him, and bid him deliver his sword, which he was loath to do; and being tied twice about his wrist, he was fumbling a great while before he would part with it; but before he delivered it, there was a runaway troop of theirs that had espied him in hold; says one of them 'My Lord General is taken prisoner'; says another, 'Sir Arthur Haselrigg is taken prisoner, face about and charge', with that they rallied and charged us, and rescued him, wherein I received a shot with a pistol, which only took off the skin upon the blade bone of my shoulder.

King Charles would later make a rare jest, commenting that if Haselrigg 'had . . . been victualled as well as fortified, he might have endured a siege of seven years.'

Meanwhile Sir William Waller had advanced with his own brigade of horse, flanking his two bodies of foot. Sir John Byron prepared to charge him, leaving

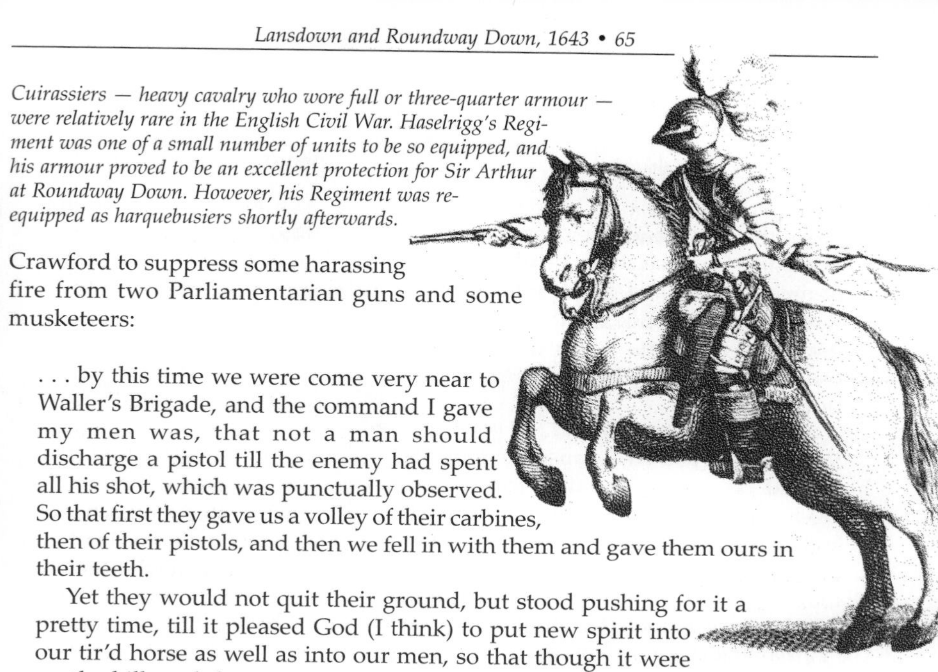

Cuirassiers — heavy cavalry who wore full or three-quarter armour — were relatively rare in the English Civil War. Haselrigg's Regiment was one of a small number of units to be so equipped, and his armour proved to be an excellent protection for Sir Arthur at Roundway Down. However, his Regiment was re-equipped as harquebusiers shortly afterwards.

Crawford to suppress some harassing fire from two Parliamentarian guns and some musketeers:

> . . . by this time we were come very near to Waller's Brigade, and the command I gave my men was, that not a man should discharge a pistol till the enemy had spent all his shot, which was punctually observed. So that first they gave us a volley of their carbines, then of their pistols, and then we fell in with them and gave them ours in their teeth.
>
> Yet they would not quit their ground, but stood pushing for it a pretty time, till it pleased God (I think) to put new spirit into our tir'd horse as well as into our men, so that though it were up the hill, and that a steep one, we overbore them, and with that violence that we forced them to fall foul upon other reserves of horse that stood behind to second them, and so swept their whole body of horse out of the field, and left their foot naked, and pursued them near three miles over the downs in Bristol way till they came to a precipice, where their fear made them so valiant that they gallop'd down as if it had been plain ground, and many of them

The steep slopes at the southern and western edges of Roundway Down which proved so disastrous for some of Waller's fleeing cavalry.

John, Lord Byron (c.1600–52) was one of seven brothers who fought for the King, Byron was one of the most effective Royalist cavalry commanders, seeing action at Edgehill, First Newbury and Marston Moor.

> broke their own and their horses' necks. In my return from the chase, I took two pieces of their cannon, and divers wagons laden with ammunition, and then rallied together our scattered troops, which were as much broken as the enemy by reason of their hot pursuit.

Waller seems to have escaped the rout, and he joined his foot. The latter formed two 'hedgehogs' and held off Wilmot's cavalry for at least an hour until they saw below them the Cornish foot at last advancing out of Devizes. Waller and Alexander Popham attempted to conduct an organised retreat, for Byron saw that the Parliamentarian 'hedgehogs'

> . . . began gently to march off, their officers marching before them amongst which (as I have been told since) Sir William Waller himself was, and Popham. With that I advanced toward them with those troops I had rallied, and shot at them with the cannon I had formerly taken. Their officers thought it not fit to stay any longer, but such as had horses rid away as fast as they could, and too fast for us to overtake them, and the rest blew up their powder, and threw down their arms and betook themselves to their heels.

Heading for the wooded eastern slopes of Roundway Down, around the earthwork now known as Oliver's Castle, some of the fugitives were cut down or ridden down in the area at the foot of the slope known as Bloody Ditch.

The Royalists' victory was complete. They claimed a total of 600 Parliamentarian dead and 800 prisoners, with 36 colours. The true total of dead may only have been about half this, but the end result was indisputable. The last major Parliamentarian field army in the West had been defeated beyond hope of recovery, and the initiative lay firmly with the King.

From Bristol to Lostwithiel, 1643–44

With Waller's army effectively destroyed, the Western forces joined a detachment from the Oxford Army under the command of Prince Rupert to attack Bristol, second city and port of the kingdom. Inadequately garrisoned, Bristol was stormed on 26 July in one of the most closely fought and bloodiest assaults of the war. Losses among the Western forces were particularly heavy. The Cornish lost perhaps 200 dead, something like a third of their total in the war so far — a savage blow on top of similar losses at Lansdown. More crippling still, however, were the deaths of two of their principal remaining original leaders, Sir Nicholas Slanning and John Trevanion. Clarendon wrote a moving tribute to them:

> They were both of them very young, neither of them above eight and twenty, of entire friendship to one another, and to Sir Bevil Grenville, whose body was not yet buried; they were hurt almost in the same minute and in the same place, both shot in the thigh with musket bullet, their bones broken, the one dying presently, the other some few days after, and both had the loyal sacrifice of their sovereign's very particular sorrow, and the concurrence of all good men.

Bristol did not, as is sometimes suggested, mark the end of the Cornish Army, but it would never entirely recover. As Mary Coate, a leading historian of Cornwall in the Civil War, explained,

> . . . the army which Grenville and Hopton had led so triumphantly across the Tamar after Stratton had perished as surely as if it had fallen with Grenville on the heights of Lansdown, or with Slanning by the walls of Bristol. For the life of the Cornish Army had been in its leaders; they had inspired it with enthusiasm, they had given it its unity, and when they died its history ended. Lansdown and Bristol might be numbered among the Royalist triumphs, but for the Cornish army they were its Ichabod.

After Bristol the Royalist forces divided. The Marquis of Hertford, after increased friction between himself and Rupert and Maurice, was honourably 'retired' to a place on the King's council at Oxford. The Oxford Army moved against Gloucester. The Western Army, under Maurice and, initially, Carnarvon, was tasked with reducing the remaining Parliamentarian garrisons in the West. Carnarvon persuaded the defenders of Dorchester, Weymouth and Portland to surrender but returned to the Oxford Army in protest at the unchecked plundering by some of Maurice's troops.

Maurice, adopting Carnarvon's conciliatory approach, headed for Exeter with a small army. The will of its defenders, who were already sealed off from outside assistance, to resist was broken by the surrender on 28 August to local Royalist forces under Colonel Sir John Digby of the northDevon towns of Bideford and Barnstaple. Exeter itself accepted generous terms on 4 September, giving the Royalists control of the 'capital city' of the West and an important administrative centre. Plymouth, its defenders discouraged and divided by treachery, might have fallen to an immediate attack, but Maurice moved first against Dartmouth, which fell on 6 October. By the time the Prince joined Digby outside Plymouth, he himself was ill and the defenders had been reinforced and resupplied by the Parliamentarian fleet. The Royalists, with Plymouth still defiant, went into winter quarters.

In the spring of 1644, his army reorganised and reinforced, Maurice, leaving a small force under Digby (and later Sir Richard Grenville) to blockade Plymouth, moved back eastwards to besiege the small Dorset port of Lyme, the capture of which would complete a line of Royalist garrisons across the neck of the south-western peninsula. Expected to be easy prey because of its weak defences and its being overlooked by high ground, Lyme proved defiant. With the aid of supplies and reinforcements landed by the Earl of Warwick's fleet, the defenders were just able to hold out against Maurice's uninspired siege operations whilst on 29 March the defeat of Hopton by Waller at Cheriton in Hampshire heralded the return to the West of the full rage of civil war.

CHAPTER III

Lostwithiel, 1644

On 17 April 1644, alarmed by the growing threat to the Royalist capital presented by the Parlimentarians following their victory at Cheriton, the pregnant Queen Henrietta Maria left Oxford, bound for the greater security of Exeter to await the birth of her child. King Charles and his advisers were uncertain about their best strategy for the coming campaign, torn as they were between concern about the danger presented in the south by the Parliamentarian armies of the Earl of Essex and Sir William Waller and the steady advances made in the north by the Scots and their Parliamentarian allies, who were now closing in on the city of York.

Robert Devereux, 3rd Earl of Essex (1591–1648)
Essex was a somewhat lethargic character, whose limited prewar military experience included service on the Continent, the Cadiz Expedition of 1625 and the First Scots War. He was personally brave, and generally popular with his men, but he had a quarrelsome nature and was quickly offended. An uninspired strategist, Essex narrowly avoided disaster in both 1642 and the following year when he allowed the enemy to get between him and his base. Unable to suppress his own real or imagined grievances for the greater good of the cause, Essex had failings that would lead him to disaster in 1644.

Philip Skippon (d.1660)
A Norfolk man, Skippon began his military career as a pikeman in the Low Countries. Returning to England in 1639, he became a military instructor to a group of London military enthusiasts known as the Artillery Garden and in 1642 was given command of the capital's Trained Bands. In 1643 he became Major-General of Foot to the Earl of Essex and distinguished himself at the First Battle of Newbury (20 September). He would occupy the same post in the New Model Army. Skippon was well likd by his troops, for whom he wrote several popular devotional pamphlets, 'with rude verses interspersed'.

Sir William Balfour (d.1660)
A Scottish professional soldier, Balfour served with the Dutch until 1627 and in 1630 was Governor of the Tower of London. Parliament's Lieutenant-General of Horse at Edgehill in 1642, Balfour had a reputation as a consistently competent and reliable soldier.

In May, in a rare example of co-operation, Essex and Waller seemed to have patched up their differences as their armies closed in on Oxford, but on 4 June, after preliminary skirmishing, Charles slipped out of the trap in a daring night march through the Cotswolds and headed for the temporary safety of Worcester. As he had probably hoped, the new-found spirit of co-operation between Essex and Waller proved to be short-lived.

On 6 June one of the crucial meetings of the English Civil War took place in the Gloucestershire town of Stow-on-the-Wold as the Parliamentarian commanders considered their next move. Essex, as Parliament's Captain-General, had the final say, and he concluded that the relief of hard-pressed Lyme was the most urgent task, and one which was best performed by his own army. The same day he informed the Parliamentarian directing body, the Committee of Both Kingdoms, that this mission was 'next to fighting with the King's army I suppose to be of most instant concernment . . . The King is now fled rather than gone . . . I have therefore applied myself to the relief of Lyme.' The disgruntled Waller, who regarded the West as his own particular area of concern, would be left to deal with what Essex regarded as the remnants of the King's forces.

Essex's civilian overlords in Westminster were far from happy with his decision. They had favoured sending Waller to the west, and on 11 June, after receiving Essex's despatch, responded by ordering him to send only a detachment of troops to relieve Lyme and to halt with the remainder until he received further instructions. These came two days later with an order to blockade Oxford.

It was, however, at least in Essex's opinion, too late for such a strategy. He had by now reached Blandford in Dorset, and on 14 June he fired off a long and petulant despatch to Westminster. He claimed that the enclosed nature of the terrain around Lyme made its relief by only a party of horse impossible, and that by marching westwards with his whole army he was in fact obeying the Committee's original instructions. Citing the support of the leading Cornish Parliamentarian magnate,

Lord Robartes, who was with him, Essex continued: 'I am commanded therefore by the discipline of war and rules of reason to march further with my foot, for fear my horse should receive a blow; I must not retreat, for then the enemy will be encouraged and strengthened.' With Robartes' support, Essex claimed that Parliamentarian sympathisers in the West Country would rally to him if he continued to march westwards, perhaps even to the relief of Plymouth. In a bitter passage, Essex was unable to conceal his animosity towards Sir William Waller:

> Pardon me, if I make bold to direct my own Major-General [Richard Browne who was at Abingdon, and receiving orders from Waller] for in that I do not see how Sir William Waller can take care of all the countries along the seaside from Dover to St Michael's Mount . . . If you think fit to set him at liberty and confine me, be pleased to make him General, and me the Major-General of some brigade, that my soldiers may have free quarter, free plunder, and fair contributions besides, as his have without control.

There was little, from far-off London, that the Committee of Both Kingdoms could actually do to gainsay their near-mutinous Captain General. They reluctantly accepted that, as Essex pointed out, 'If you call back Sir William Waller from pursuing the King and stop me in my march to the west, we are likely to lose the benefit of both armies this summer.'

Other commanders, notably the Earl of Warwick, heading the Parliamentarian fleet that was assisting the defenders of Lyme, believed that Prince Maurice's besieging army to be so worn down that a force of 1,000 horse and 600 dragoons would be sufficient to relieve the town. His opinion seemed confirmed on 15 June when Maurice, with only 2,500 foot and 1,800 horse left out of his original force of about 7,000 men, abandoned the siege and retreated towards Exeter, which he reached three days later.

Essex sent his Lieutenant General of Horse, Sir William Balfour, with a party of cavalry to confirm that Lyme was safe and followed up his advantage by occupying Weymouth, on 19 June, and Bridport. From newly captured Weymouth, after meeting the Earl of Warwick, an optimistic Essex assured Westminster:

> I am informed by the Lord High Admiral that the Western Counties will flock in from all parts to our body, in case I advance with my army further West. Plymouth men will take the field with two thousand five hundred horse and foot, and fall upon the rear of the enemy, whilst we charge them in the front. Lastly it is the unanimous judgement of the joint council of war, both by sea and land . . . that it will be exceeding prejudicial for me to retreat or only make a stand; and that my advance will (in all human reason, by the blessing of Heaven) be effectual for the preserving of Lyme, breaking the Enemies' Association and reducing the west.

On 25 June the Committee of Both Kingdoms reluctantly acquiesced in the inevitable by giving their Captain General a free hand to conduct operations as he wished, though they voiced their displeasure at his attitude:

> . . . if the Resolutions of the House, and the Directions of the Committee . . . had been followed, the Public Affairs had been in a better Condition than now they are; especially in these Parts. And we are also to let your Lordship know that in Your Letters . . . of the 14th, 16th and 17th of this instant, June . . . there are many Expressions [that] might well have been foreborn, and do not question but you do now wish they had not been written. But to make the best use of their Affairs as they now stand, they find themselves necessitated to use New Counsels, and would have your Lordship to take all Advantages on the Enemy, and use your best Endeavours for reducing the West.

By now the first seeds of doubt seem to have been sprouting in Essex's mind, when, from Chard on 25 June, he informed his political masters that Maurice's forces were larger than he had anticipated and that Lord Hopton was actively recruiting for the Royalists in Somerset. However, these concerns were insufficient to alter Essex's resolve to advance at least far enough westwards to relieve Plymouth, and he counted on Sir William Waller to protect him from pursuit.

Unbeknown to the earl, this hope was about to be shattered. Far from being a broken fugitive, as Essex had professed to believe, King Charles had outmanoeuvred Sir William, returned to Oxford and picked up the remainder of the Oxford Army before, on 29 June, turning the tables on Waller at Cropredy Bridge in Oxfordshire, inflicting on him a sharp reverse which effectively put Sir William's army out of action for the remainder of the summer.

With the immediate crisis over, the King and his councillors could consider their next move. They were uncertain of the outcome of Prince Rupert's attempt to relieve York, and during the early days of July, with contradictory rumours of the result of the great battle of Marston Moor (2 July) filtering through, the Oxford Army, with about 2,500 horse and 5,000 foot, moved slowly westwards through the Cotswolds.

The king's overriding concern remained the safety of his wife and her newborn daughter in Exeter. Essex had refused them safe conduct, and it was plainly his intention to capture them for use as bargaining counters or worse. These considerations played a major part in discussions regarding what strategy the Royalists should now adopt. On 12 July the king's Secretary of State, Lord George Digby, wrote to Prince Rupert that contradictory reports of Marston Moor meant that the King and his commanders:

Robert Rich, 2nd Earl of Warwick (1587–1658). An underrated figure, Warwick , appointed Lord Admiral of the Parliamentarian navy in 1642, proved to be a consistently competent commander.

King Charles I.

> ... know not what judgement to make of it, nor how to govern our counsels in order to your Highness's condition ... We cannot come time enough to assist you, nor, though we could, could we hope to maintain or preserve our armies in the march. There remains nothing for us to do but to go westward, since your Highness have not had good fortune in your late action, we should be cooped up and have no way out of Wales to the West. Prince Maurice has a gallant army, equal with Essex ... If we get to join with him before Waller overtake us, we shall be likely to crush him between us. If Waller press in hard, we hope that with the forces which may meet us out of Bristol, and with the help of the recruits, to be sent thither out of Wales, we may make our party good with him and Browne [at Abingdon] in case they join again.

By 15 July the King had reached Bath. He knew that Waller was out of immediate contention, currently in the Midlands in the neighbourhood of Daventry. The more immediate concern was Essex, with an army of about 3,000 horse and 6,000 foot, who was known to be in the vicinity of Exeter. Maurice, with between 5,000 and 7,000 men, still desperately stripping the neighbouring garrisons for more troops, felt unable to meet Essex in battle unless he was joined by the King and on 18 July fell back to Crediton.

Although Charles did not yet know it, the Queen was now safe. Not wishing to run the risk of being trapped in Exeter, Henrietta Maria, escorted by a troop of horse under Major Edward Brett — travelling because of her still fragile state of health by horse litter — had been taken to Falmouth, from where, on 14 July, narrowly escaping the attentions of the Parliamentarian navy, she took ship for the safety of France.

Essex's Plan

Essex meanwhile had reached Tiverton in Devon on 5 July. Here he received news of the King's march into the west and called a Council of War to consider his course of action. There appeared to be three options. First, he could turn back and meet the King in Somerset. Secondly, he could lay siege to Exeter. The third choice was to continue west, relieve Plymouth and reduce Royalist Cornwall. The first option might result in Maurice taking the Parliamentarians in the rear as they prepared to fight the Oxford Army, whilst Exeter was known to be provisioned for two months and was thus unlikely to fall before the King arrived.

The outcome was that Essex decided to continue westwards. He believed that the small force of Cornish troops under the despised Parliamentarian defector Sir Richard 'Skellum' Grenville, the unprincipled younger brother of Sir Bevil, which was currently blockading Plymouth, would disperse as the Parliamentarians approached, whilst Lord Robartes was promising widespread support in Cornwall. Rather unadvisedly, Essex was relying upon Waller or other unspecified Parliamentarian forces to harry the rear of the pursuing Oxford Army and cut off its supplies.

Essex did in fact have better reasons for his choice than is often suggested. He had enjoyed some success in his march so far. Apart from relieving Lyme and taking Weymouth, he had also occupied Taunton, and the always pro-Parliament town of

Barnstaple in northDevon had passed back into the hands of the Roundheads. Whilst Essex had to rely on Robartes' assurances regarding the degree of support he was likely to receive in Cornwall, he was fully aware of the importance of the county to the Royalist cause. The capture of the Cornish ports, whose exports of tin and imports of munitions were vital to the King's war effort, was a prize for which it was worth taking risks.

At first all seemed to be going well, though on 10 July, in an ominous hint of what was to come, Essex admitted to the Committee of Both Kingdoms: 'I confess that the country has suffered somewhat of late for want of the soldiers' pay.'

Prince Maurice remained unable to counter the Parliamentarian advance. He called a rendezvous at Okehampton of Royalist forces in the West, apart from Grenville's regiments of horse and foot and some new Cornish levies, which were left to maintain the blockade of Plymouth. In Cornwall the Royalist activists Sir Francis Bassett and Joseph Jane tried to raise the Cornish *posse comitatus* but met with little success. Cornish morale had slumped after the flight of the Queen as well as on reports of Essex's approach, and, as usual, those levies which actually appeared refused to cross the Tamar. Jane admitted that 'our labours were to persuade the men to go into Devon, telling them it were better to fight before the country was invaded, which gained some credit, but not strongly enough to move the body, who twice turned back in a strange mutiny.'

Eventually about 1,500 of the posse were bribed or persuaded to join Maurice. On 6 July the Prince had mustered a total of about 2,000 horse and 5,000 foot, including 800 foot from Bristol and 1,000 Somerset levies raised by Ralph Hopton. His intention initially was to bring Essex to battle, and on 18 July he advanced to Crediton, but, learning that the King was now within four days' march, he decided to join Charles, and 'with their Forces united to make the Game the surer.'

Charles and the Oxford Army had meanwhile been marching through Somerset by way of Bruton and Ilchester. On Tuesday 23 July the King had called a muster of the county militia on Kingsmoor near Ilchester, though only about 200 of them, placed under the command of Sir Edward Rodney, proved willing to join the Royalist army; the rest 'having seen their sight, went home again.' On 24 July the Royalists moved on to Chard, and next day to Honiton, before joining Maurice on 26 July outside Exeter. The general apathy of

Sir Richard Grenville (1600–58), brother of Sir Bevil, was a hard-bitten and unscrupulous professional soldier, who after serving in Ireland, defected from the Parliamentarians to the Royalists, earning the deep enmity of his former employers.

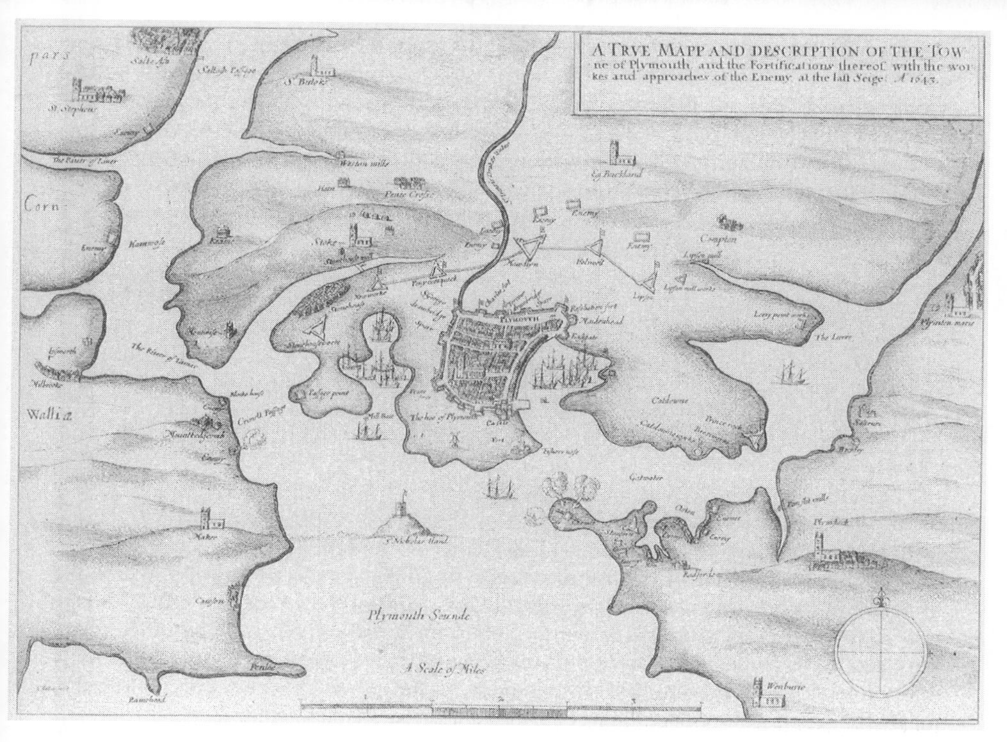

The defences of Plymouth in 1645.

the West Country people towards both sides continued. Only a handful of the Devon Trained Bands proved willing to enlist with the King, and he suffered an annoying reverse when a party of raiders from Lyme beat up the quarters of Lord Percy's Regiment of Horse.

By now the Earl of Essex was reported to be within seven miles of Plymouth, and the combined Royalist armies continued in pursuit, on the 28th arriving at Crediton — uncharitably described by Captain Richard Symonds, an officer in the king's Lifeguard of Horse, as 'a great lousy town.' The Royalist Council of War found it difficult to believe that Essex would march into Cornwall and thought it more likely that, having relieved Plymouth, the earl would attempt to return eastwards through south Devon, and Prince Maurice issued orders for bridges in that area to be broken down. At the same time measures were taken to set up a supply system for the Royalist armies with provisions to be despatched from Somerset and Devon. Sir John Wake's cavalry brigade from the Western Army was stationed at Chard to escort convoys.

As they marched, the Royalists were obtaining increasing evidence of the indiscipline and destructive activities of Essex's men. Two local churches had been vandalised, 'a great rick' of oats had been burnt and local people had had large sums of money stolen. Such activities were not, of course, the monopoly of either side, but the Royalists were making strenuous efforts to curb looting by their soldiers, one of whom was hanged for such an offence on 29 July, at Bow — 'a small and contemptible Village', in the view of Sir Edward Walker, Charles' supercilious Secretary at War.

Essex, meanwhile, had arrived at Tavistock on 23 July. Grenville, with fewer than 2,000 men, hastily abandoned the blockade of Plymouth and fell back across the Tamar into Cornwall. Rather unwisely, he left a small garrison in his own house near Tavistock. Essex sent out a party to deal with it, and

> . . . at their approach those within hung out a White Flag, and desired a Parley, but the Soldiers eager for Pillage went on, and stormed it; and getting over the Wall entered the House, whereupon all the Defenders cried for Quarter, which was granted to all but Irish Rebels. Here were taken two Pieces of Cannon, one hundred and fifty prisoners, a great quantity of Muskets and Pistols, and Money, Plate etc to the Value of Three Thousand Pounds.

Grenville was soon to lose more than his personal property. He had pulled back his troops to defend the crossing of the Tamar at Horsebridge, aware that he was unlikely to be able to halt a determined attack by the enemy. Essex, meanwhile, despite doubts by some of his officers, had heeded Robartes' urgings and decided to press on into Cornwall, 'to clear the country and settle the same in peace.' It is hard to justify his decision. Parliamentarian numbers had already been significantly depleted by the need to find garrisons for Weymouth and Portland, and lack of pay and the march into unfamiliar territory were causing desertions not compensated for by the small numbers of Devon Parliamentarians who enlisted.

War Returns to Cornwall

The Parliamentarians were now entering what was clearly — despite Robartes' optimism — hostile territory. The Cornish had for a long time been regarded with suspicion by most Englishmen, and by 1644 Parliamentarian propaganda aimed at them had hardened to a point at which the Cornish were compared with the hated Irish. The result was that Essex's men immediately began to behave in a manner which assured hostility. Threats were made that no quarter would be given to any

King Charles I (1600–49)

As the younger son of James I, Charles had not been expected to ascend the throne, nor was he trained in kingship. He was handicapped by a speech impediment, and by his aloof and uninspiring personality. His belief in the 'Divine Right' of kings led Charles to attempt to impose his system of Personal Rule, which, with his unpopular religious policies, helped bring about Civil War.

He had no military training, and was hindered in generalship by a devious and frequently irresolute character, though he displayed personal courage of a somewhat passive kind. He did, however, learn some skills through practical experience, and the campaign of 1644 was his outstanding — indeed, arguably his only — military success.

Patrick Ruthven, Earl of Forth (c.1573–1651)
'A hail man, born for the hardship of Soldier', Patrick Ruthven was one of the numerous professional soldiers produced by seventeenth-century Scotland. He served with the Swedes for the next thirty years, and was greatly valued by King Gustavus Adolphus, not least as a man 'who could drink immeasurably and preserve his understanding to the last' — hence his nickname 'Pater Rottwein'.

Ruthven fought for King Charles in the Scots Wars and was created Earl of Forth. In 1642 he became Lord General of the Oxford Army, playing a leading role in its operations during the next two years, though by 1644 ill-health, gout, deafness and the effects of wounds had somewhat incapacitated him.

Cornish, one result of which was that most of the male population fled from the towns and villages on Essex's line of march. The earl commented apprehensively, 'through many towns and villages where my army passes, there is none but women and children.' His soldiers worsened the situation by the way in which they 'vaunt over the poor inhabitants of Cornwall as if they had been invincible.' It was not long before hatred sharpened into active enmity. One Parliamentarian soldier commented that the Cornish were 'so base . . . that if any of our soldiers chance to straggle abroad, a great number of the country people meet with them . . . and cut their throats.'

At first, however, Essex's operations seemed to be going according to plan. On 26 July he sent a party to attack Grenville's position at Horsebridge. The Royalists do not appear to have put up very serious resistance; indeed, Sir Edward Walker claimed that Grenville evacuated his position without a fight. In fact there seems to have been a sharp skirmish in which the Parliamentarians lost forty or fifty men and Grenville rather more, perhaps as many as 200, before the Royalists retreated. Essex occupied Launceston, capturing forty barrels of powder, and two days later, on 28 July, entered Bodmin.

Parliamentarian news reports claimed that Royalist resistance in Cornwall was on the point of collapse. Many of Grenville's men were reported to be surrendering, whilst Sir Richard himself 'flies like guilty Cain from every shadow, frightened by his fancies and tormented by a prickling, galled conscience for symptoms of misery, a hell within and a halter at Westminster that makes the man as mad as a March hunted hare.'

Whilst there certainly was a loss of morale among the Cornish Royalists, a number fleeing overseas, Grenville was not in quite the dire straits depicted by his opponents. Sir Edward Walker wrote that 'Sir Richard Grenville, like a man of honour and courage, kept a good body together and retreated in good order to Truro endeavouring to raise a force sufficient to oppose Essex's further advance . . .'

George Goring (1608–57)
Goring was a wild youth who, after falling heavily in debt, took refuge in military service on the Continent. Joining the English troops in Dutch service, he took part in the Siege of Breda (1637), suffering an ankle wound that left him semi-lame for the rest of his life, but he returned home something of a popular hero.

A born intriguer, Goring adopted a somewhat ambiguous attitude at the start of the Civil War, when he was Governor of Portsmouth, before declaring for the King. On Portsmouth's surrender he went to Holland, then became General of Horse in the Earl of Newcastle's Royalist forces in the north of England. After a brief but dramatic career he was captured at Wakefield (21 May 1643) and then spent a year as a prisoner before being released in time to lead the Northern Royalist cavalry with distinction at Marston Moor.

Goring was an outstanding cavalry commander,but his greater potential was undermined by drink, ill-health and an unprincipled love of intrigue.

Grenville was making energetic efforts to recruit his forces, including the seizure of horses from suspected lukewarm Royalist supporters such as the Earl of Bath. However, he was still too weak to face Essex and retired westwards from Truro to Penrhyn, where he issued warrants calling out the *posse comitatus*, though with limited results. Only news of the approach of the combined armies of King Charles and Prince Maurice would restore Cornish confidence in the Royalist cause.

On 30 July the King's forces arrived at Okehampton and next day reached the eastern bank of the Tamar at Liston, where Charles and Maurice examined the bridges broken down by the Parliamentarians and presumably ordered repairs. A messenger arrived from Grenville to report, with considerable exaggeration, that Sir Richard now commanded a force of 8,000 men; the King sent him back to Grenville and 'bid the fellow tell him he was coming with all possible speed with an army of 10,000 foot, 5,000 horse and 28 piece of cannon.' On the same day Royalist troops crossed the Tamar and entered Launceston, effectively placing Essex in a 'Cornish mousetrap'.

The news of the King's approach reached Essex on 2 August at Bodmin, and he reacted by moving south towards Lostwithiel and Fowey, where he could keep open communications with the Earl of Warwick and the Parliamentarian fleet. Essex was becoming increasingly alarmed, and wrote to the Committee of Both Kingdoms on 4 August:

> . . . we now hear that three armies are marching against us from the east under the command of the king, of the Palgrave Maurice, and Lord Hopton, while nobody so far as we can hear are attending on them and the country rising unanimously against us, with the exception of a few gentlemen. We must expect another army upon our backs from the west. This prospect with the great necessity of the soldiers, who want bread, has forced me to choose this place to make good till we can be provided with victuals from Plymouth, or

> hereabouts, to enable us to march. Then we shall sell our lives at as dear a rate as may be, for I have never seen soldiers more willing to undertake anything nor to undergo wants with more patience . . .

The Royalists, meanwhile, were steadily closing in. On 3 August the King ordered Grenville to advance from Penrhyn to Tregoney, near Grampound, in order to hinder Essex from foraging in that direction. The King and his advisers were keenly aware of the need to gain the support of the local population, and Charles issued a proclamation to his troops telling them that they were 'entering a country exceedingly affectionate to His Majesty'. Violence and looting directed against the civilian population was forbidden, and food convoys from Somerset were introduced in an attempt to supply the Royalist forces.

Whilst these measures would have only partial success, and some looting undoubtedly did occur, the Cornish regarded the King's forces as decidedly the lesser of the evils which they faced. Evidence of their support was soon apparent. On 2 August, after rendezvousing on Coryton Down, the combined Oxford and Western Armies advanced to Liskeard. Their aim was to begin to reduce 'the Rebels to Necessities for want of provisions', and in this the King's men were assisted by the local population. Large numbers of country people were coming into the King with news of enemy movements 'to please his worship', and the first Parliamentarian prisoners began to be taken. At Liskeard, two Parliamentarian officers were captured, said Richard Symonds, one of them, known as 'Will of the West', being a well-known wrestler and carpenter and the other a London pewterer. The same night a captain of horse with twelve of his troopers was taken at St Clear, and the following day more prisoners were brought in: 'amongst the rest two women took one.'

Lostwithiel, showing the bridge over the River Fowey in the foreground and St Bartholomew's Church in the centre.

As this contemporary cartoon of an English soldier in Ireland demonstrates, looting was a universal habit among seventeenth-century soldiers.

On 4 August

> . . . some of the country people came and complained to the King that the enemy was a plundering of the country and desired aid. The King sent a party of horse of Colonel [Richard] Neville's Regiment, commanded by Sir Bernard Gascogne, an Italian, who troops with Colonel Neville, and the colonel went with him as a volunteer. They met with a boy who told them of a many of gay men in the Lord Mohun's house [Boconnoc]. Notwithstanding they had eighty musketeers to guard them, as they were carousing they forced the doors upon them, killed the man that locked the door, broke in the house, took Colonel Aldridge who was governor of Aylesbury, the Lieutenant-Colonel, captain and one ensign of Essex his life-guard, another Lieutenant-Colonel, without the loss of any one of his Majesty's party. This house was within two miles of Essex his headquarters. Dalbier, a Dutchman, Quartermaster-General of Essex his army and engineer, was in this house with those rebels, but put off his sword and hat, and pretended to be a servant to the house of my Lord Mohun, and so escaped.

Walker adds more details of the exploit: Neville 'made haste thither presently, forced the Gates, and got Possession of the Dining Room. They still kept a Buttery at the end of it, until through the Door one of their Servants was slain; then they rendered themselves Prisoners.

The King Closes In

The King's forces had now been reinforced by about 100 of the Cornish Trained Bands, and during the next few days Royalist pioneers opened up the narrow, steep-banked and hedged lanes leading from Liskeard towards Lostwithiel so that the artillery could be moved along them. On 7 August the Royalist forces marched from Liskeard to Pinnock Down, where they quartered in the vicinity of the battlefield of Braddock Down in the previous year.

Some skirmishing took place in the course of the day between scouting parties of the opposing sides. The Royalists were already experiencing difficulties with troops straggling away from the colours, and four Royalists were killed (presumably by the enemy) when bringing in provisions; another man suffered the same fate when he was sent out to bring in 'rambling soldiers'. The King, with Prince Maurice and their Lifeguards of Horse, spent the afternoon on the crest of Braddock Down looking down over Boconnoc towards Lostwithiel, the bulk of their foot stationed at the base of the hill in the vicinity of Boconnoc itself. Charles returned to Liskeard to spend the night, his Lifeguard on the alert around the town — 'where we watched on horseback', remembered Symonds.

Charles had other decisions to make that night. For some time his Lieutenant General of Horse, Henry, Lord Wilmot, had been exhibiting increasing signs of discontent and disagreement with Royalist policy. He was suspected to have been in treasonable communication with the Earl of Essex, though in fact Wilmot was probably guilty of little more than meddling in political matters which were not of his concern. In any event Charles, who had a long-standing dislike of Wilmot, had for some time been seeking an opportunity to replace him. His successor, chosen with the support of Prince Rupert, was to be George Goring, a sometimes drunken intriguer but also a brilliant cavalry commander, who had been the only senior Royalist to come out of the débâcle at Marston Moor with any credit. He arrived hotfoot from the North at Liskeard that evening, and next morning the King prepared to make his move.

As Wilmot drew up at the head of his troops on Braddock Down he was arrested by the King's Marshal at Arms and charged with treason. The astonished cavalry troopers were informed that their new commander, at the request of Prince Rupert, was to be George Goring. The result was some discontent, with Goring himself expressing concern to Rupert about the mutinous attitude of some of his new command. However, following a petition from the officers of horse to the King, and an explanation by the latter of reasons for Wilmot's arrest, matters settled down

Lanhydrock House. The home of the Cornish Parliamentarian Lord Robartes, Lanhydrock was largely rebuilt after a major fire in the nineteenth century.

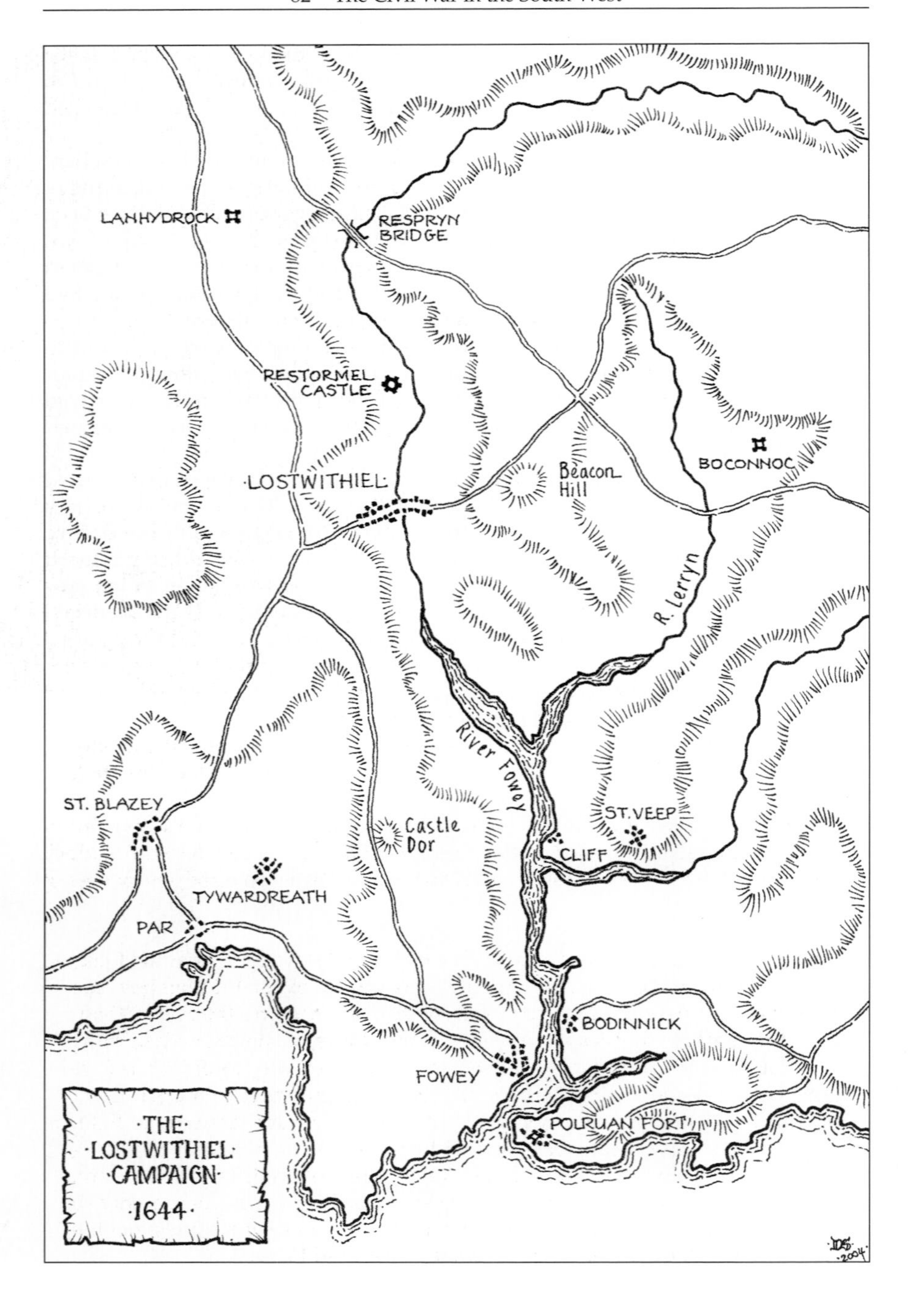
LANHYDROCK
RESPRYN BRIDGE
RESTORMEL CASTLE
LOSTWITHIEL
Beacon Hill
BOCONNOC
R. Lerryn
River Fowey
ST. BLAZEY
Castle Dor
ST. VEEP
CLIFF
TYWARDREATH
PAR
BODINNICK
FOWEY
POLRUAN FORT
THE LOSTWITHIEL CAMPAIGN 1644

A portrait of George, Lord Goring (1608–57)

fairly quickly. Wilmot was eventually allowed to retire to France without being charged with what were almost certainly acts of stupidity rather than treason.

This difficulty resolved, further skirmishing took place during the day. A forlorn hope of 1,000 picked musketeers from the Oxford Army under Colonel Matthew Appleyard 'went off the heath through a lane between enclosures to another heath called by the same name near the enemy'. This was the position which had been occupied by Hopton's army at the start of the battle of Braddock Down in 1643.

In the afternoon, Symonds relates,

> Divers great parties of our horse beat the enemy's horse quite off the hills within view of Lostwithiel, the headquarters of Essex. We took some prisoners, five or six killed on both sides in piquering [skirmishing]. Some of their foot was seen this day near the town of Lostwithiel in the closes; parties only of their horse met some of ours.
>
> Towards night the body of the King's foot were moving towards the Enemy near, but, growing night, retired half a mile back to the bottom of another hill.

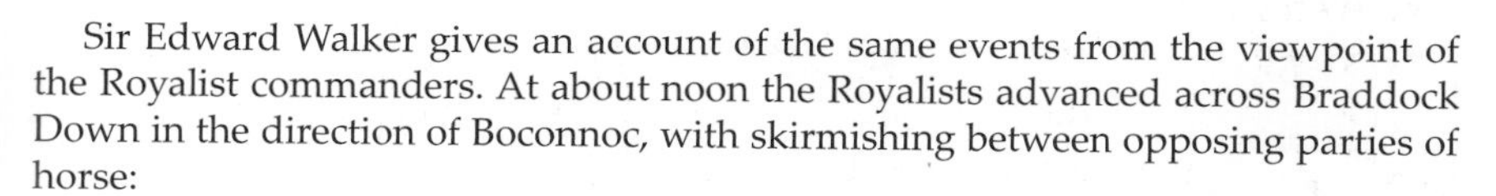

Sir Edward Walker gives an account of the same events from the viewpoint of the Royalist commanders. At about noon the Royalists advanced across Braddock Down in the direction of Boconnoc, with skirmishing between opposing parties of horse:

> Then we drew up our Army in good Order and sent stronger Parties of Horse, who presently made the Rebels quit that part of the Heath which lies between Boconnoc and the Lord Mohun's Warren, they still keeping the Hill without Boconnoc Park. In this Posture we stood some Hours, facing each other, being very cautious how we engaged ourselves, though I am very confident had we gone on that Time we had in human Probability put them to retreat, if not obtained a Victory. For our Men were full of Courage, and desirous to fight; they on the contrary were surprised with our advance, and our Army being ranged on the Top of a Hill at the best Advantage, put great Terror into them. But it was not our play, having through so many Difficulties got together so good an Army, to engage it on an uncertain Issue, for as yet we knew not the Ground they stood on, nor the Advantages they had there.

That night the Royalists camped on the heath, with the King resting in the midst of his army.

Next morning, 9 August, saw a renewed debate about whether the Royalists should attempt to bring on a battle that day or bide their time. 'The last was concluded on as sufficient and most for present Advantage, as well to refresh our Horse, who had been on great Duty, as to expect Sir Richard Grenville, who was noised to be coming towards us with 8,000 Horse and Foot.' This decision did not preclude all activity, however, and Richard Symonds was a keen eyewitness of the day's events. At about 8 a.m. the main body of the Royalist foot moved in the direction of Lostwithiel, and about two hours later

> Some of their foot came out of the town and hill. They shot two piece of cannon at half an hour after ten at ours.
>
> Prince Maurice his army had the van this day, and marched towards my Lord Mohun's house in the park of Boconnoc between the house and the Lord Robartes's house called Lanhydrock, both houses being but four miles apart.

Some further cavalry skirmishing took place, when 'a commanded party of our horse met with some of the enemy, but loosely retreated without charging. No business of note done, some soldiers came in, some taken.'

During the day Grenville had advanced through Grampound, and in the evening he occupied Bodmin after a brief skirmish with Parliamentarian horse.

Essex at Bay

The King was hopeful that Essex, realising the difficulties which he now faced, and resentful at lack of support by Westminster, might be prepared to agree to terms. A message to that effect had been sent to him by Charles on 7 August, and during the evening of the 10th was followed by a further appeal signed by Prince Maurice and the Earl of Forth as generals of the two main Royalist armies. Essex, perhaps not surprisingly, remained defiant, and replied tersely:

> My Lords,
>
> In the beginning of your letter you express by what authority you sent it. I having no authority to treat without the Parliament who have entrusted me, cannot do it without breach of trust.
>
> Your humble servant,
>
> Essex.

Essex could say little else, but the mood in the Parliamentarian camp was increasingly anxious as they awaited news of any relief attempt.

As early as 24 July the Committee of Both Kingdoms had ordered efforts to be made to assist Essex, but the problem lay in finding troops to attempt the task. With the bulk of Waller's army unfit for action, and at a halt around Farnham in Hampshire, all that Sir William could provide was a force of 2,000 horse and dragoons under his Lieutenant General of Horse, John Middleton, a Scottish professional soldier. The hope was that Middleton might be able to disrupt the Royalist supply convoys in Somerset and so force the King to march back eastwards. The Committee of Both Kingdoms voted a sum of £20,000 to be used to purchase provisions for Essex, which were to be despatched by sea in the charge of the experienced Captain Richard Swanley. However, by 9 August a London newspaper, the *Parliament Scout*, was admitting that the 'Lord General was in great straits'. On 18 August Parliament voted another £18,000 for Essex's army, but the problem of conveying it to him remained.

Middleton's expedition was never more than a forlorn hope, and came to grief on 14 August, near Bridgwater in Somerset, when Middleton encountered a similar sized Royalist force under Sir Francis Doddington and Sir William Courtney, who were escorting supplies to the King's armies in Cornwall. According to the version of events in the Royalist newspaper, *Mercurius Aulicus*, Doddington

> . . . sent a good number of Musketeers before, to line certain hedges where they knew Middleton was to pass; and afterwards sent two Carriages slenderly guarded, as a bait for the greedy Scot, which Carriages he quickly seized upon, and with them was hasting homewards through a long narrow lane five miles from Bridgewater [*sic*], but there he received such sudden unexpected salutes from the Musketeers on both sides the Hedges, that he faced about in much haste and confusion, and then the two Knights fell so gallantly on him, that they broke his whole Party all to pieces, killed fourscore in the Lanes, and took 140 Prisoners, whereof Major Carr (that renegade Scot) was one . . . the two Carriages regained, which (with all the rest) are conveyed safe to His Majesty's Army; Middleton with his scattered Rebels sufficiently bruised, retreated back to Sherbourne in Dorset.

The view from Beacon Hill looking eastwards towards Druids Hill, now more heavily wooded than in 1644. This was the scene of some of the initial fighting in the campaign.

Even before he received this good news — which meant that any chance of Essex being relieved by land had effectively disappeared — the King had continued slowly to tighten his grip on the Parliamentarians. On 10 August Grenville, continuing his advance eastwards, took Respryn Bridge and Lanhydrock House without resistance and met up with Lord Hopton and 2,000 horse and foot on Cardinham Down. The Royalists, with a total strength of around 18,000 men, were now united and had Essex hemmed into an area extending from just above the small town of Lostwithiel down the river valley to the port of Fowey. The Fowey valley was commanded on either side by hills averaging 400 feet in height. If those overlooking Lostwithiel and Fowey were to be lost, the Parliamentarians would be doomed. The King's commanders — probably under the overall command of the Oxford Army's vastly experienced Lord General, the old Scottish professional soldier Patrick Ruthven, Earl of Forth — felt, however, that the Parliamentarians were still strong enough to withstand a direct assault until they were weakened by lack of supplies, and for some days operations were designed mainly to restrict their opportunities for foraging. King Charles had now made his headquarters at Boconnoc, and in the afternoon of 11 August he and his commanders met there with Sir Richard Grenville to confer about their next actions.

A trickle of deserters confirmed that morale was sagging in Essex's army, and on 12 August the Royalists attempted to capitalise on this by scattering papers on the

Respyrn Bridge.

This view of the entrance to Fowey harbour illustrates how it was commanded by the Royalist battery at Polruan.

heath between the opposing quarters, offering pardon to any who submitted, though at this stage they met with little response.

The Royalist commanders had by now concluded that

> . . . if we did not block up the River at Fowey, to hinder the bringing in of Provisions by Sea, and keep the Passes on that River and Creek, between our Quarters and that Town, to hinder the Rebels' Excursions, we might lie long enough where we were, and instead of starving the Rebels be starved ourselves.

Tightening the Net

Thus troops under Sir Jacob Astley, Major General of Foot in the Oxford Army, and George Goring were sent to take control of the eastern bank of the River Fowey, especially 'Hall', Lord Mohun's house at Bodinnick Ferry, Penruan Fort at the mouth of the river opposite Fowey, and St Veep Pass. In a major error, Essex made no attempt to oppose this operation and Hall and Polruan were garrisoned by 200 Royalist foot with two or three guns under Lieutenant Colonel Richard Page of Sir James Pennyman's Regiment. Symonds recounted with obvious relish that in the course of the operation Astley had captured 'two butts of sack, much tobacco and horseshoes etc conveying from Fowey to the enemy.' The only routes by which supplies from the sea could now reach Essex were via the small port of Par and a few coves below the cliffs at Menabilly.

On 14 August Grenville, supported by 2,000 of Maurice's foot, began closing in on the enemy on the western side of the River Fowey. Lanhydrock House was occupied, many bows and arrows, relics of the Tudor militia, being found there. One of Maurice's soldiers was hanged for looting, for, despite being the home of Lord Robartes, Lanhydrock had been given protection.

The fort at Polruan from which Royalist guns could close the entrance to Fowey harbour.

By now what to later generations of holidaymakers might have appeared a typical Cornish summer had begun. Symonds described 15 August as 'a blustering cold day and the evening very wet.' The change in the weather, if it were to prove prolonged, might have caused problems for the Royalists, many of whose troops must have been billeted in tents or huts in the open, but the King's Secretary of State, Lord George Digby, remained confident, writing that day to Prince Rupert that

> The Earl is certainly possessed with such a frenzy as nothing can come but that ruin which certainly he is destined whichever side soever prevail. . . . I make no doubt but that all the ill-humours in our Armies will be well allayed now that the two poles upon which they moved [Wilmot, and Lord Percy replaced as General of Ordinance by Lord Hopton on 14 August] are taken away.

The wet weather continued next day, during which Royalist troops gradually spread their net further around Essex's position. Two deserters came in to report that the Parliamentarians were running short of provisions.

On 17 August King Charles personally inspected the enemy position across the river from the terrace at Hall, having a fairly narrow escape when a fisherman standing nearby was decapitated by a cannon shot. At around the same time Essex was writing bitterly to the Committee of Both Kingdoms:

> If any forces had followed the King, as we expected, when we came into these parts, in all probability the war would have had a quick termination. . . . Braver

men I never knew [but] this army being environed by four armies [leaves] us in a great want of victuals, and the country so obstructed by passes, that we can neither force the enemy to fight except when they wish, nor march off ourselves. For ought I can perceive the enemy's intention is to starve us out, yet both our horse and foot keep their courage notwithstanding the great extremity they are put to. The foot as yet have never been engaged, but the horse skirmish daily, and invariably beat their opponents though they be three for one.

Intelligence have we none, the country people being very violent against us, and if any of our scouts or soldiers fall into their hands, they are more bloody than the enemy.

However the Royalists, with major problems keeping their forces supplied with food and ammunition by means of convoys coming from as far as Dartmouth and Exeter, were concerned by their seemingly slow rate of progress. On 18 August a Council of War was called at Boconnoc:

For as yet we saw little Fruit of the Posture we were in, and less Prejudice done to the Rebels; therefore it was unanimously concluded that we should draw all our Horse and Foot out of our Quarters, and Sir Richard Grenville should do the like from Lanhydrock, and then march nearer to the Rebels on every side; and either engage them to fight, or place our Quarters so near them, as to keep them to greater Duties, or to take other Opportunities when we should see the Place wherethey lay.

The Battle of Beacon Hill

The first objective for the Royalists would be the ground overlooking Lostwithiel, with its highest point at Beacon Hill. Essex had earlier placed a large detachment of infantry in Fowey, with the remainder of his foot around Lostwithiel and the ruins of Restormel Castle a mile to the north of the town. The castle had been built to cover Lostwithiel and its bridge, the lowest road crossing of the River Fowey before it reached the sea. However,

Jacob, Lord Astley (1579–1652). A blunt professional soldier, Astley was a highly capable Major General of Foot during the Scots Wars and continued to demonstrate his ability in this role with the Oxford Army.

'Hall', home of Lord Mohun near Bodinnick. Now a farmhouse.

on 21 August there appear to have been no Parliamentarian troops occupying Beacon Hill itself.

The Royalists' plan was for a simultaneous advance on a four-mile front on both banks of the river between Lanhydrock and Boconnoc. At about 5 a.m., covered by early morning mist, the armies of Charles and Maurice were drawn out of their quarters, and two hours later they marched to the top of the high ground on the north -eastern side of Lostwithiel, overlooking the town and flanking the road to Liskeard, where the main force stood all day, supported by the Earl of Cleveland's brigade of horse.

At the same time Grenville advanced to occupy Restormel Castle. This was supposed to be defended by the Devon Parliamentarian foot regiment of Colonel John Weare, but on a day on which nothing went right for the Parliamentarians there was evidently a misunderstanding between Weare and Essex: some of the earl's subordinates had apparently not been informed that the Castle had been garrisoned.

According to Richard Symonds,

> Sir Richard Grenville . . . with 700 men on the other side [of the river] pelted the rogues from their hedges between the Lord Robartes his house at Lostwithiel and near Trinity [Restormel] Castle . . . which castle was this morning surprised by Sir Richard Grenville's men and some thirty of the rebels taken and divers barrels of beef.

Essex himself, with his highly capable Major General of Foot, Phillip Skippon, was at Lostwithiel, whilst Major General Holbourne and Colonel Fortescue were in command against Grenville. However, the Parliamentarians' reactions were slow and unco-ordinated.

A commanded party of 1,000 musketeers from Maurice's Western Army now occupied a hill about half a mile to the north side of Lostwithiel:

> . . . the small cottages which were on this hill next the town were all this forenoon a burning. Our foot and theirs pelting one at another all day. Small harm done to ours. The enemy shot a many great pieces of cannon at them and at the left wing of our horse; little or no hurt. Thus stood both armies all this day on this side.

'These Places being thus possessed,' wrote Sir Edward Walker, 'we then had leisure to survey the manner of their Quarters, and (seeing they would not draw out) to resolve where to make our own. . . . All this while the Rebels did very little by way of Opposition, and were certainly surprised.'

In the afternoon Essex belatedly began despatching more horse and foot to oppose Grenville in the fields north of Lostwithiel. Sir Richard seems to have fallen back a short way.

> Many skirmishes there were between ours and them, they regaining some Fields that we had taken, and had certainly done more, had they not been stopped by two gallant Charges made by two small Bodies of our Horse. The first commanded by Major James Smith [with troops of the Western Army],

Restormel Castle, although partially ruined by 1644, was still a potentially useful defensive position.

High ground east of Lostwithiel occupied by the Royalists.

> who routed a Party of their Horse, and charged their Foot up to a Hedge lined with Musketeers, who all gave fire upon him; where notwithstanding he came off in good Order, and kept his Ground without Loss, himself being shot in the Arm. The other Charge was made by Sir Robert Walsh [Lieutenant-Colonel, Sir George Vaughan's Regiment] upon their Foot, and some Execution done upon them, yet I believe the number slain that Day was not above forty Persons of Both Armies.

Essex's version, unsurprisingly, was rather different. He described later how, 'within musket shot', he had placed

> Lieutenant-Colonel Ingoldsby with four hundred Musketeers, and fronted with my Regiment, and Colonel Tryell's regiment, the Orange Regiment for reserve, the Lord Robartes and Colonel Barkley's on a Hill on the left hand in the same time, and upon them Prince Maurice lay with his Army. The Major-General's [Skippon's] Regiment between mine and them; in the Town Colonel Weare's men; the River ran under the Town, and he was to guard a Passage at a Gentleman's House, not two Musket-Shot from the regiment, and an old Castle lay over it, which they quitted at the first appearance of the enemy. On a Hill on the other side of the Town, towards Bodmin, lay Major-General Hethcote's Regiment, and Lieutenant-Colonel David's Regiments, and out of the regiment most of our Musketeers upon the Passes, which Ware's men lost, and our Forlorn Hope took most of our Musketeers. Against the regiments on Bodmin's side lay Grenville's Army at the Lord Robarte's house.

Losses were relatively light because, with the exception of the two Royalist cavalry charges, there seems to have been little close-quarter fighting. The troops of both sides had largely remained under the protection of the steep banks and thick hedges of the numerous small fields, exchanging often ineffectual fire.

As evening came on, the Royalists began to go into quarters; however, in the most significant action of the day, a brigade of Oxford Army foot gained possession of the hills on either side of the valley running down to Lostwithiel. Those on the left, near the Chapel of St Nectan, were guarded by Appleyard's 1,000 'commanded' musketeers from the Oxford Army whilst Maurice's Western foot took up position on the right. During the night the Royalists constructed a 20-yard-square fort on the summit of Beacon Hill and emplaced several light guns there.

Essex's reaction throughout the day had been feeble. This was partly because he was concerned by his low stock of ammunition, which narrowly escaped a major disaster when the Royalists attempted to blow up his main magazine,

> . . . for which purpose, into two Wagons filled with Barrels of Powder there were two Engines privately conveyed, and put amongst the Barrels, and were so near doing Execution that the lighted Match that was fastened to the end of one of the Engines was burnt within an inch of the Wild fire, where it was discovered, and the other Match was burnt to the very Neck of the Engine where it was to give fire, but it happened not to take, and so the Coal was gone out of itself.

'In Great Extremities'

Dawn broke on 22 August with Essex, apparently blaming Colonel Weare's evacuation of Restormel for his situation, in a position of disadvantage. His troops in Lostwithiel could be fired on by the Royalist battery on Beacon Hill.

The day was spent by the Royalists in consolidating their gains. Maurice's men continued to occupy the higher enclosed ground which they had gained the previous day; the Oxford Army foot were in the enclosures on the southern side of Boconnoc Park, to the east of Maurice and separated from him by about half a mile of heathland. The bulk of Essex's men were in front of Lostwithiel, drawn up on two areas of rising ground, 'the one opposite to our new Fort, and the other to Prince Maurice's

This view north-westwards from the summit of Beacon Hill towards Lostwithiel demonstrates how the hill dominates the approaches to the town.

The coastline south-west of Fowey harbour. Only a few small supply ships could make use of the coves in this area.

Quarters, and within little more than Musket shot from either.' The bulk of the Royalist horse lay to the west, in the direction of St Blazey. According to Richard Symonds, 'This day was maintained in all parts what we had got in the night, many of the enemies' great shot of 9lb being shot at our men. One of our cannon shot luckily at a party of enemy's horse and killed two horse and one horse's leg shot off at once.'

Next day also dawned misty, and Symonds observed that

> The work on the top of the hill aforesaid next the said chapel seemed in the misty morning to the enemy to be a body of horse, as some of their sentries were heard to say. They shot a piece of 9 lb many times at this work, killed one and hurt another; that was all the hurt was done us this day at the work. On Sir Richard Grenville's side Colonel [Phillip] Champernown of Devon, colonel to Prince Maurice, Leading up his men near Trinity Castle, was shot in the neck; his own men took off his sword and cloak and left his body, which the enemy took; since by a drummer we hear that his wounds is not mortal.

Throughout the day, King Charles, escorted by his Lifeguard of Horse, rode around inspecting his troops: 'Then we returned to our quarters in the field, as the two nights before; mornings and evenings being very misty; through the night starlight.' Also on 23 August, in order to limit Essex's foraging area still further, George Goring was sent with 2,000 horse and 1,500 foot under Sir Thomas Bassett westwards towards St Blazey and Par.

Essex was now penned up, with approximately 10,000 men, in an area measuring about five miles by two, running from Lostwithiel to Fowey, and with only a few coves in which to land supplies if the continuing stormy weather allowed Parliamentarian ships to approach. Many of his troops, Essex, claimed, had been in constant action following the loss of Beacon Hill: 'From the 21st until Friday seven night after, most of the Foot on Bartlett's side, and the side next Bodmin, was in continual fight. I had but sixty Musketeers with my colours, and never able to relieve them all that time.' On 27 August he admitted in a despairing letter to the Committee of Both Kingdoms:

> . . . our duty here is so great that if the enemy do not draw off or we receive succour speedily, we shall be put to great extremities, spending much ammunition and match, which we cannot afford, besides the fatigue of the soldiers, many of them not having been relieved for eight days. . . . Had I known that Waller, who was to attend the King's army, had wanted either power or will to have a care of it, no persuasions of those who are interested in these counties should have engaged me so far in a country so ill-affected to the Parliament.

It was rather late in the day for regrets of that kind, and Essex's men were feeling increasing despair. One soldier wrote on 28 August: 'We are amongst a people as far from humanity as they are from sanctities, for they will neither serve God nor man, but after the old fashion of their grandfathers.'

King Charles, however, had concerns of his own. The operation to reduce Essex was taking longer than had been expected and Charles 'had good reason to endeavour to bring it to a speedy Issue; for his Army, (especially the Cornish) was much diminished, Provisions grew short, and Middleton was then coming on our backs.' Though the latter fear was unfounded, there was certainly good reason for hastening the pace of operations. On 24 August there were briefly hopes that Essex

This contemporary view of the seventeenth-century Army of Flanders shows vividly the effects of long campaigning on the dress of the soldiers.

had begun pulling back from Lostwithiel. Symonds wrote that the usual ineffective Parliamentarian bombardment of the Beacon Hill battery took place that morning: 'No harm: we got many of their bullets.' At 3 p.m. the King was back on the hill, 'and divers came and told him the enemy was gone towards Fowey, for indeed none or very few of them could be seen; about two of their cannon played some time, and some muskets; almost all that were there beside the King and Prince Maurice were of opinion they were gone.'

Grenville and the Western foot had been readying themselves to attack, seconded by the Oxford Army infantry. However, closer examination demonstrated that the Parliamentarians, though under cover, were still in position, and the Royalists decided to mount a major attack next day. The King favoured the idea, feeling it 'not to be so difficult as was conceived' by some of his commanders. It may be, however, that some of the doubters dragged their feet, for next morning nothing went according to plan. August 25 dawned yet another wet and windy day, but King Charles was in position on Beacon Hill by 3 a.m. and

> ... presently sends word to the Prince his army to know if they were marching, and to tell them he was here and ready, and that he conceived it a fit morning to do the business, likewise he sent the like to Sir Jacob Astley, to tell his own army so. Preparations on all parts of the King's side: his horse are come into the field, half of them gone over to Sir Richard Grenville's side. An [hourly] expectation of our readiness to fall on. Prince Maurice about twelve of the clock comes armed and tells the King he was ready, and asked the King if he were so; immediately their resolution altered, and our troops were sent to Liskeard. Long before this was evident enough, that the enemy was not gone, only well hid from the danger of our battery, but was tout prepare to receive us.

Some of the apparent Royalist dithering that morning may have been caused by concern about ammunition supplies: it was not until the following day that a large ammunition convoy arrived from Dartmouth and Pendennis, bringing with it 1000 barrels of powder.

After the Royalists sent Goring and his detachment towards St Blazey, Essex

> ... was forced to send Colonel Behr with my Regiment[of Horse], his and the Plymouth Regiment, with five hundred Musketeers, to defend the Passage.
>
> If in all this time but five hundred Musketeers had been sent us, we should have ventured to have beat up one of their Quarters: but if we had lost a hundred men as we were, we must have quitted one of our posts, and then we had been Ruined ...

Essex's position was not perhaps quite as dire as he conceived it to be. With all but 500 of his cavalry absent, either with Goring or guarding the roads from Plymouth, the King's forces were dangerously spread out guarding a perimeter of fifteen miles. The uncertain nature of communications over so wide a front had probably helped cause the problems encountered on 25 August and made a renewed attack difficult.

Balfour's Escape

In the event, Essex moved first. The Parliamentarian Council of War resolved on 30 August that, with supplies of fodder almost exhausted, the 2,000 horse under Lieutenant General Sir William Balfour should attempt that same night to break out and head for Plymouth. The Royalists were informed of the enemy plan at seven o'clock in the evening by two deserters, but they either suspected the reliability of their informants or had too little time to make adequate preparations. However, warnings were sent to George Goring (who, at St Blazey, was too far away to do anything), to the small force of horse under Sir Edward Waldegrave (who was guarding the approaches to Saltash, still held by the Parliamentarians) and to the garrisons at St Veep and Polruan. The most vulnerable point was correctly seen to be the junction of the Oxford and Western Armies on the road from Lostwithiel to Boconnoc, and a cottage here was garrisoned by a detachment of fifty musketeers.

Balfour needed more luck than the Parliamentarians had so far encountered in the campaign, and for once he got it. Setting out at about 3am on 31 August, he was aided by a particularly dark and misty night. The outpost of Royalist musketeers either amazingly failed to hear the hooves of the Parliamentarian cavalry as they passed by their cottage, or decided that discretion was the better part of valour. In any event, they failed to raise the alarm. Balfour was spotted soon afterwards by patrols from the Earl of Cleveland's brigade of horse, but with only 250 men immediately available, Cleveland could not prevent the break-out. All he could do was round up a few stragglers, and then, at dawn follow Balfour with orders to observe him but not to engage until reinforced.

As Cleveland tracked the Parliamentarians across Coryton Down he was joined by 100 men of Sir Thomas Aston's regiment of Horse and 150 Cornish Horse under Captain Mohun, not nearly enough for him to risk a serious engagement. Some skirmishing did take place, during which Major Dundas of Cleveland's Regiment was wounded and briefly captured. The Parliamentarian Captain Abercromby was trapped in a house with twenty of his dragoons, and held out until a party of the King's Lifeguard of Foot arrived, who, with the aid of some country folk, forced the doors and captured the Parliamentarians. The remainder of Balfour's force, with the loss of no more than 100 men, got clean away into Saltash and thence by boat to Plymouth as the Royalists abandoned the pursuit at nightfall.

Confusion and recrimination in the Royalist camp were rife. It was not until daylight that the King had clear information

Sir William Balfour (d.1660) A Scottish professional soldier, Balfour was appointed Lieutenant General of Horse in Essex's army in 1642.

concerning Balfour's intentions, for some time fearing that the Parliamentarian horse intended to form up in the cover of the woods and then attack the Royalist quarters. The Earl of Clarendon would later blame Goring for the débâcle, alleging that he had been drunk and had ignored the alert which had been sent to him, but in fact it is apparent that Goring received no instructions to follow the enemy until well into 31 August, by which time it was far too late for him to catch up with Balfour.

The breakout had been almost inevitable, given a situation in which the Royalist forces were spread so thinly. Indeed, if he had been prepared to abandon his artillery and wagons, Essex might have stood a good chance of extricating his foot along with his horse.

The Battle of Castle Dor

Essex, with some 8,000 foot, remained firmly in the Royalist trap. At the same time as Balfour and the horse began their breakout, Essex began to pull his foot and guns back towards Fowey, in the faint hope that the Earl of Warwick might evacuate them by sea. He soon ran into difficulties. There were clear signs of a breakdown in discipline among some of his troops, who looted and made an unsuccessful attempt to blow up St Bartholomew's Church in Lostwithiel together with some Royalist prisoners who were confined there.

Parliamentarian disorganisation was increased by the recent heavy and prolonged rain, which had left the narrow lanes and tracks thick with mud. Essex complained:

> The ways were so extreme foul with excessive rain, and the harness for the draught horses so rotten as in the marching off we lost three demi-culverins and a brass piece, and yet the Major-General [Skippon] fought in the rear all day, he being loth to lose those pieces, thirty horse were put to each of them, but could not move them, the night was so foul and the soldiers so tired that they were hardly to be kept to their colours.

Lostwithiel Bridge.

The Royalists, stung by the escape of Balfour and the Parliamentarian horse, were determined that Essex's infantry should not get away. Having ordered up Grenville and Goring from the west with all speed, the King, escorted by his Lifeguard of Horse, was in the field early; Richard Symonds was with him:

In this interim his Majesty lost no time, but with those foot he had (which God knows were very few, most of them being straggled abroad the country for provision), and with his own troop and the Queen's, marched towards Lostwithiel. On the hill next beyond the town were bodies of the enemies' foot with colours left in their rear to make good their retreat: their baggage, artillery, and the rest of Essex his foot army having marched all the night towards Fowey.

The King, observing the Parliamentarian foot pulling back from Lostwithiel to 'some high fields towards Fowey', sent a party of foot into the town to drive off some of the enemy who were attempting to break down the bridge over the river there. As the Royalists occupied the town, Grenville's men were advancing through the neighbouring fields and found that near Creek 'that comes up from thence about half-a-mile on their left hand and in the Fields where they drew up beyond that town [the Parliamentarians] left two Demi-Culverin being excellent Pieces, and a little further two other Pieces and some Ammunition.'

King Charles and his Lifeguard rode through Lostwithiel, and then left the Cornish foot to head the pursuit, 'who were quickly in the rear of the Rebels' Army, and from Hedge to Hedge forced them to a hasty Retreat.' Symonds, riding forward with Charles, noted that after the Royalist forlorn hope of foot — possibly Appleyard or Maurice's commanded musketeers — had entered Lostwithiel

> . . . his Majesty had commanded 2 or 3 pieces of cannon to be placed in the enemy's leaguer to command the hill where their foot reserve stood, the enemy's reserve marched away, our forlorn following them in chase from field to field at a great pace. About 8 of the clock his Majesty with the two troops passed over the river on the south side of Lostwithiel, where the enemy had left a cartload of muskets, besides many more in the dirt a little higher, 5 pieces of

St Bartholomew's Church, Lostwithiel. The eastern side of the spire still bears signs of the explosion.

> cannon in several places, 2 of them being very long ones. With this small force his Majesty chased them 2 miles, beating them from hedge to edge.

By now the Parliamentarian rearguard had fallen back to the higher ground between Tywardreath Bay and St Veep, and here Essex, with his own, Lord Robartes, Skippon's and Bartlett's Regiments of Foot, made a stand.

The earl described how he

> . . . took two Troops of the Plymouth Horse that were on St Blazey side, and Colonel Butler took a hundred Musketeers, and Captain Lloyd all of my Regiment, and the two Troops fell upon three or four of the Enemy's Regiments and their Horse, beat them back two or three closes; Butler that was released [exchanged after being captured at Boconnoc on 4 August] but the day before fell into the midst of them, and took a Red Colour; the Plymouth Horse with Reynolds in the head of them, charged bravely, twenty of the King's Horsemen quitted their Horses, and ran through the Closes. Captain Reynolds is a gallant young Man, and was shot through a narrow-brimmed Hat with a Musket Bullet, and one of the Troopers took another foot colour, which put us in some Comfort.

Essex may have telescoped events somewhat, but the Royalist Sir Edward Walker admitted that

> . . . at length the Rebels having got some Advantage of the height of Ground and some Enclosures made a stand, and with some few Horse forced our Cornish to a very hasty and unhandsome Retreat; to quit the Fields they had

Castle Dor from the west.

High ground with small, enclosed fields south of Lostwithiel, in the area where the Parliamentarians made their initial stand.

> got, and retire to a body of our Foot, commanded by Lieutenant-Colonel [William] Leighton [King's Lifeguard of Foot] who made good his Ground, and rallied them again.

It was now about 11 a.m., and in this fierce fighting in the hedgerows west of Trebathevy Farm the Royalists seemed to have been brought to a halt, being particularly hindered by enemy musketeers firing from the cover of the thick hedges and steep banks. The King had very little cavalry available to support his infantry, but

> . . . about 11 of the clock Captain [Edward] Brett led up the Queen's Troop, and most gallantly in view of the King charged their foot and beat them from their hedge, killing many of them, notwithstanding their muskets made abundance of shot at his men: he received a shot in the left arm in the first field, and one of his men, La Plunne, Frenchman, killed, yet most gallantly went on and brought his men off; his cornet's horse shot, with 2 other horses, and 2 more wounded. He retreated to be dressed, and the King called him and took his sword which was drawn in his hand and knighted Sir Edward Brett on his horse's back. This was just at 12 of the clock. About this time we took 7 or 8 prisoners, whereof one was a captain of foot, who was taken by Captain Brett's men, and another took one of their cannoniers, who was pitifully drunk, having shot off his cannon but once.

Walker claimed that 'If we had had but 500 Horse at that time with the Foot, I believe we had utterly defeated them; and truly had the Rebels but that number there, we had been put to Straits, and our Victory would have been more Difficult.'

A short lull followed until about 2 p.m.,

> About which time all of our Body of Foot was come up, and the Van led by Colonel Appleyard and Colonel Leighton advanced and charged the Rebels.
>
> The Lord Bernard [Stuart, King's Lifeguard of Horse] with his Troops seconded them; for three of their Troops (being all the Horse they had) charged

our Foot; but upon the Lord Bernard's Approach they retired, and our foot gained much Ground.

Symonds also witnessed these events:

> . . . now the King's foot came on apace and increased much. Shooting continued much on both sides, more on theirs, we still gaining ground. About 4 of the clock some of the rebels' horse (they having 2 or 3 troops with them), charged our foot, but the Lord Bernard immediately got leave of the King to draw up his troop, who were all ready, and drew up to the rogues, standing their musket shot a long time; but, because their horse retreated and their foot lay so close under the hedges, which are all cannon proof and have no avenues wider than one or in some places 2 horse can approach at a time, and likewise because his Majesty sent to draw us off, we fairly retreated, one of the Queen's troop was here killed. More of our foot coming up to relieve the rest.

At about 4 p.m. General George Goring, not having learnt of Balfour's escape until 10 o'clock that morning, arrived on the scene with more of his horse and the Royalist advance continued. By 6 p.m. the Royalists were approaching the high ground around the Celtic earthwork of Castle Dor: 'Now was our foot in great bodies got upon the high hill just in the narrowest passage of land between Trewardreth parish church and the passage over the river which runs by Lostwithiel.'

By this time the Parliamentarians were firmly at bay. If they lost their line of defence running across the neck of high ground between St Austell Bay and the River Fowey, centred on Castle Dor, their situation would be desperate. At about 6 p.m. they made another determined counter-attack. Symonds admitted:

> Just about 6 of the clock the enemy made a very bold charge both of cannon, muskets and horse, to gain this hill[where the Royalist foot were positioned], as likewise the pass near St Veep, but were valiantly beat off, and our men not only keeping both but got some ground also. This heat lasted about an hour; at first it was so hot that the Lord Bernard drew out his Majesty's troop with the colours (for the time before we left them with the King) to charge the rebels, but General Goring met us and told him the room was too little for [his] horse and our troopers to charge too, and advised he would please to face a little and draw off to the King. Here was of the Queen's Troop one shot in the shoulder. With our troop was drawn up the Queen's, Prince Maurice his life guard commanded by [the earl of] Arundel, and the Lord Hopton's which was commanded by Sir Thomas Wilford, of Kent; these made a brave body of about 200, all well armed.

The actual task of halting the Parliamentarian attack fell to the Earl of Northampton's brigade of horse, but it took about an hour of hard fighting before, at about 7 p.m., the Parliamentarians were forced back to their position at Castle Dor, on the final ridge of high ground overlooking Fowey. In the centre, the ancient earthwork of Castle Dor commanded the roads running eastwards towards Golant, westwards

The view northwards from the Parliamentarian position at Castle Dor towards the ground across which the Royalists advanced.

to Tywardreth and southwards to Fowey and Menabilly. The remaining Parliamentarian guns were positioned in the earthworks, with Colonel Butler and Essex's own Regiments of Foot on the left. The vital eastern flank of the position, covering the road to Golant and the river, was held by Colonel Weare's Devon Regiment and those of Lord Robartes and Colonel Bartlett.

Essex claimed that, by now,

> . . . coming to the ground-fighting all the way, the ground could not be chosen to best advantage, and the poor Soldiers instead of being eased of their Duty, were in such a place as that the enemy might bring every man of ours to fight; and they far surpassing us in Number, it might easily be judged how they could [resist] tired out with continual Duty. The train was placed upon a Hill in the midst; on the right side of the River that comes from Fowey was my Regiment, Ware's men (or rather Sheep) and Bartlett's and the Lord Robartes. The enemy pressed hard upon them; Colonel Butler… came and told me, that Robartes' and Bartlett's men had quitted their Posts, and gone two Fields back; Wear's men flung flung down their Arms, and ran away. My regiment seeing themselves left, do what Butler could, marched up to the Train.

Essex's account is primarily concerned with excusing himself and sheds little light on what actually happened. Later some of his officers, led by Philip Skippon, wrote their own version of the day's events. They had fallen back towards Fowey

> . . . with such Difficulty, by reason of the Steepness of the Hills and the deepness of the Ways, that five of our Cannon were lodged, which retarded our March till the three Armies surrounded us, and caused a continual fight for three miles together upon our retreat; wherein our Soldiers behaved themselves so

Castle Dor. The ancient defences still presented a significant obstacle to attackers.

> resolutely, that we did often beat the Enemy back to their Body, and took three of their Foot Colours, and five and twenty Horse, and about three-score Prisoners. So that if we had any fresh men to have spared from our Posts (wherein the whole Army was upon continual duty) we should in all probability have had a great advantage upon the enemy. . . . Butler seemed very unwilling to draw his men to the place assigned, which occasioned [Skippon] to tell him that he wondered to see him so unwilling and again commanded him to the said Place. That afterwards Colonel Weare came to Skippon and told him he could not maintain his Post. . . . Skippon sent him back and bid him to maintain it as long as he could. . . . And afterwards, it being dark, Colonel Butler came in like manner, and told him he could not maintain his Post, because he could not keep above two hundred Men together, and that therefore he had drawn off the Regiment. Skippon did not know then or since, that any Man was slain there at that Place, and saith that none of the King's Party did press upon that Post to possess it but the same was free the next Morning, and that there was not above fifty of the Enemy that had pressed at that time upon that Post.

Whatever the reason for the Parliamentarian collapse, it evidently came unexpectedly. Walker said that Weare's men, on Essex's eastern flank, suddenly began marching down towards the river bank, 'either resolving to have fallen on our Flank, or securing their own Passage.' It may indeed have been a desperate attempt by some of Weare's Devon men to escape from the trap, but if so it was doomed to failure. Weare's troops were isolated, and a general collapse, occasioned by exhaustion and discouragement, was now spreading amongst the Parliamentarian foot. According to Walker, 'but finally their Main Body retreated, and some of our Foot making towards them, they at first made a stand, but presently after began to stagger, and in great Disorder to quit that Field, and run back with their Cannon and Colours towards their main Body.'

It was not, in other words, a complete rout, and although Walker estimated that total losses on both sides for the day were no more than 200 men, exhaustion and the gathering darkness made the Royalists conclude that they had achieved enough for one day. As Symonds described, the opposing forces were still within musket range of each other and some firing continued during the night:

> The King sending for us [the Lifeguard of Horse] to come to him, and the enemy's volleys abating and ceasing, we were drawn in the next close but one where his Majesty was. And this was the chief of the business of the day. Now did many of the enemy's cannon give fire at our men, till dark night. I saw a fellow of ours dressed, a musketeer who was shot in the chin, the shoulder, and the hand by cannon at one shoot. This night the King lay under the hedge with his servants in one field. The troops of lifeguard lay in the next it being very windy, and cross wind for Essex shipping of his men, and rained much and great storms. I saw 8 or 9 of the enemy's men dead under the hedges this day. Some shooting continued all night.

Despite his uncomfortable sleeping arrangements, King Charles was probably quietly jubilant at the result of the day's fighting. Not so the Parliamentarian commanders. Their troops, clustered around their baggage train on a hillside, were almost trapped, with the roads to Golant, Fowey and Menabilly effectively closed to them. It seems that Skippon had been effectively in command during the closing stages of the fighting, and the reasons for Essex's absence soon became clear. Two hours after dark, without informing Skippon or other senior officers of his intentions, Essex, accompanied by Lord Robartes and Sir John Merrick, slipped aboard a fishing smack and headed for the safety of Plymouth.

Essex spent a good deal of time afterwards in attempts to justify his action. He had, he pleaded, 'thought it fit to look to myself, it being a greater terror to me to be a slave to their contempts than a thousand Deaths', whilst 'he had rather fall into

The view eastwards from Castle Dor towards the ground occupied by Weare's Regiment.

the hands of God than Man, for if the enemy should take him, they would use him shamefully.' He assured Parliament: 'It is the greatest Blow that ever befell our Party. I desire nothing more than to come to Trial. Such losses as these must not be smothered up.'

To Phillip Skippon, left to salvage what he could from the disaster, Essex wrote effusively from Plymouth on 2 September:

> Be assured no worldly thing should have made me quit so gallant Men, but the impossibility of subsisting. . . . Sir, If you live I shall take as good Care of you as of my Father if alive; if God otherwise dispose of you, as long as I have a drop of Blood, I shall strive to revenge yours and the Causes of it... Nothing but fear of Slavery, and to be triumphed on, should have made us have gone.
>
> Yours to Death,
>
> Essex

Unfortunately, salty old Skippon's reaction to this professed devotion remains unrecorded. In somewhat more colourful terms, he might well have agreed with the comment of the Royalist newspaper, *Mercurius Aulicus*: '. . . we desire to know the reason why the rebels voted to live and die with the Earl of Essex, since the Earl of Essex hath declared he will not live and die with them?'

Early in the morning of Sunday 1 September, Skippon called a Council of War of his remaining officers, and commented briefly but acidly of Essex's departure:

> Gentlemen, you see our General and some Chief Officers have thought fit to leave us, and our Horse are got away. That which I propound to you is this; that we having the same courage as our Horse had, and the same God to assist us, may make the same Trial of our fortunes and endeavour to make our way through our enemy as they have done and account it better to die with Faithfulness than to live dishonourable.

Failing that, Skippon proposed that the Parliamentarians should form up around their powder train and threaten to explode it unless they were given reasonable terms. None of his commanders, however, had the stomach for further resistance, and the decision was taken to ask the King for his terms.

The Royalist Council of War had met the same morning and decided against an immediate resumption of their attack, resolving instead to spend the day clearing gaps through the hedges in preparation for

Philip Skippon.

a new assault the next morning. It would not prove to be necessary, as Symonds described:

> This Sunday, the rebels being within but a little compass of ground (being surrounded by sea on three parts, and our army on the land), and because their rebel General the Earl of Essex, Robert Deveraux, and their Field Marshal, the Lord Robartes, with many others of their chief commanders, had left them, and went by sea, as they supposed, or they knew not which way. Skippon, now left in chief, being Major General, sent propositions of treaty to his sacred Majesty, who out of his abundant mercy, notwithstanding having them all in so great advantage, was pleased to give them leave to march away with these Conditions:
>
> Leaving all their Cannon which were in all 42, and 1 mortar. All their muskets and pikes. . . . All their carriages except one to a regiment. To march away with their colours, and foot officers with their swords. Those officers of horse with swords, hatbands and pistols.
>
> A wagon full of musket arrows, 100 barrels of powder.

Other accounts suggest that a total of forty-five cannon, and 9,000 muskets and pikes, were captured.

During the morning of Monday 2 September Skippon and the wretched survivors of his army marched away past the triumphant Royalists. Symonds displayed little sympathy for their plight:

> . . . his Majesty's army of foot stood on the same ground or thereabouts as before, the several regiments by themselves, and the colours stuck in the ground flying, His Majesty in the field accompanied with all his gallant cavaliers dispersed in several places.
>
> While about 10 of the clock, Major [General] Skippon, first or in the front, marched with all that rout of rebels, after the colours of their several regiments. These regiments I took note of after three or four had passed.
>
> Colonel Lord Robartes
> Colonel Bartlett
> Colonel Aldridge, blue colours with lions rampant or
> Colonel Davies, white colours City London
> Colonel Cunningham, green colours
> Colonel Whichcote, green, Cityy London
> Colonel Weare [argent?] Governor of Lyme
> Colonel Carr 11 ensigns or, distinctions blue
>
> These are Plymouth men. They had more foot.
>
> Colonel Layton, a regiment of horse, blue cornets. All their ensigns and cornets were wound up, veloped [*sic*].
>
> It rained extremely as the varlets marched away, a great part of the time.

> The King himself rid about the field and gave strict command to his chief Officers to see that none of the enemy were plundered, and that all his soldiers should repair to their colours which were in the adjoining closes. Yet, notwithstanding our officers with their swords drawn did perpetually beat off our foot, many of them lost their hats, etc.
>
> Yet most of them escaped this danger till they came to Lostwithiel, and there the people inhabitants and country people plundered some of their officers and all, notwithstanding a sufficient party of horse was appointed by his Majesty to be their convoy.
>
> They all, except here and there an officer (and seriously I saw not above three or four that looked like a gentleman) were stricken with such a dismal fear, that as soon as their colour of the regiment was passed (for every ensign had a horse and rid on him and was so suffered) the rout of soldiers of that regiment pressed all of a heap like sheep, though not so innocent. So dirty and so dejected as was rare to see. None of them, except some few of their officers, that did look any of us in the face. Our foot would flout at them, and bid them remember Reading, Greenland House (where others that did not condition with them took them away all prisoners) and many other places, and then would pull their swords, etc, away, for all that our officers still slashed at them.
>
> The rebels told us as they passed that our officers and gentlemen carried themselves honourably, but they were hard dealt withal by the common soldiers.

King Charles, typically ineffectively, was greatly distressed by the behaviour of his troops. When Sir Edward Walker, who claimed that the plundering only occurred because some of the Parliamentarians were carrying concealed weapons, jested that 'our soldiers freed them from their clothes.' Charles retorted angrily: 'Fie, that is ill-said and was worse done!'

The Parliamentarians' troubles were only just beginning. There were those among the Royalists who suggested that the terms granted had been too lenient, and that Essex's men should have been taken prisoner. The King, however, with perhaps no more than 5-6,000 of his and Maurice's foot still with their colours, was in no state to risk a continuation of the fighting — and, in the event, it made little difference.

Under the terms of the surrender, those Parliamentarians fit to march were to be given safe escort to their garrisons at Poole and Wareham whilst the sick and injured were to be taken by boat to Plymouth when fit enough to travel. However, it became clear from the moment that the march began that the King would be unable to fulfil his part of the bargain. A Parliamentarian complained that 'We were inhumanly dealt with, abused, reviled, scorned, torn, kicked, pillaged, and many stripped of all they had quite contrary to the Articles. . . . for even in the presence of the King and their General they took away our clothes, coats or hats.' Skippon, whom the King unsuccessfully urged to change sides, protested furiously.

Worse followed. In Lostwithiel, angry Cornish, both men and women, eager for vengeance, fell on the Parliamentarian troops and their camp followers, killing a number of them. As Symonds noted with satisfaction,

A seventeenth-century baggage train. This could consist of scores or even hundreds of wagons.

> This was a happy day for his Majesty and his whole army, that without loss of much blood this great army of rascals that so triumphed and vaunted over the poor inhabitants of Cornwall, as if they had been invincible, and as if the King had not been able to follow them, that 'tis conceived very few will get safe to London, for the country people whom they have in all the march so much plundered and robbed, that they will have their pennyworths out of them.

The ordeal continued for the next three days, as many as 300 men a day reportedly dying from the hardships of the march or at the hands of country people avenging the looting they had suffered a few weeks earlier. The Parliamentarians had neither food nor shelter and slept as best they could in the hedgerows. At Okehampton they were finally able to purchase a small amount of food at high rate from the grudging townsfolk, and from Tiverton, which they reached on 6 September, the march was a little easier. Even so, it was only through the efforts of Skippon that a handful — perhaps 1,000 out of 6,000 — finally reached the safety of Portsmouth.

Charles stayed little longer. By 4 September the Royalist armies were marching eastwards, leaving Cornwall once again secured for the King's cause.

From Lostwithiel to Langport, 1644–45

The victory at Lostwithiel seemed to offer King Charles a brief opportunity to complete his triumph in the West by capturing Plymouth. But Charles, partly because of the poor state of his army, did not wish to incur the heavy casualties likely to result from a full-scale assault. The defenders, now under the vigorous command of Lord Robartes, rejected the royal summons to surrender and by 14 September the King was marching away eastwards, eventually to confront the Parliamentarian armies at Newbury — and narrowly escape disaster.

Sir Richard Grenville was left to conduct operations against Plymouth. With his characteristically ruthless approach, 'Skellum' Grenville had a good deal of success in building up an army of respectable size and at times pressed the defenders of Plymouth severely, although the major assaults which he attempted in February 1645 were repulsed.

Grenville claimed confidence in ultimate success, but events in the wider theatre of war now overtook operations around Plymouth. Following the indecisive conclusion of the 1644 campaign, both King and Parliament set out to reorganise their war efforts. In the case of Parliament this would take the form of merging the existing major field armies into the New Model Army under Sir Thomas Fairfax, in what would ultimately prove to be the decisive action of the war.

The Royalists' measures were much less effective. Prince Rupert was placed in overall command of their armies, but he proved able neither to push through the reforms which were needed nor to exercise control over many of the King's quarrelsome and self-seeking commanders. The West was taken out of his effective control almost immediately by the King's decision early in 1645 to set up a Council of the West under the nominal leadership of the 15-year-old Charles, Prince of Wales. Part of the intention here was to 'unboy' Charles, and in March 1645 he was sent to take over his new authority, accompanied by a team of the King's most experienced advisers. The result was chaos. The Council's attempt to reinvigorate the flagging Royalist war effort by means of a new 'association' of the Western counties, which were to raise a new field army, quickly ran foul both of war-weariness and of opposition from the existing Royalist commanders in the area. Matters were worsened in the spring by the arrival in Dorset and Wiltshire of several thousand horse and foot under the command of Lord George Goring. These nominally came under Rupert's authority, but Goring, determined to exercise an independent command, played the Prince and the Council of the West off against each other, with King Charles failing to resolve matters.

By now the Royalist priority in the West was to reduce the stubbornly resisting Parliamentarian garrison at Taunton, and throughout the spring the Council of the West made unavailing attempts to persuade their squabbling commanders to co-operate in this task. Goring , when not fending off ineffective relief attempts by Waller and Oliver Cromwell, had taken command of the siege unto himself, but Grenville, ordered eastwards from Plymouth with most of his troops, and Sir John Berkley, commanding at Exeter, refused to operate under the command of the interloper and as a result the siege failed to make any progress.

Goring and his veteran cavalry were urgently needed by the King and Rupert for the main summer campaign, but Goring continued to intrigue and prevaricate. His aim now was to be recognised as *generalissimo* of the Western Royalist forces and eventually, in May 1645, he achieved this; but his refusal to place the greater good of the Royalist cause over his own interests meant that King Charles and the Oxford Army met the New Model Army in the climactic clash of the war at Naseby (14 June) without Goring and his men. Their presence might well have changed the outcome of the battle, but, as it was, Naseby ended with the almost total destruction of the King's infantry.

The Oxford Army destroyed, Fairfax and the New Model Army could turn their attention to the Royalist Western heartlands.

CHAPTER IV

Langport and Torrington, 1645–46

The victory of the New Model Army at Naseby is usually, with hindsight, seen as dealing the fatal blow to the Royalists in the First Civil War. But this was far from obvious at the time, nor necessarily inevitable. Much hard fighting still lay ahead, with a recovery by the King's cause not to be ruled out. Though most of the veteran foot of the 'Oxford Army' had been killed or captured at Naseby, the King and Prince Rupert had managed to salvage about 3,000 horse from the disaster and Charles had retired with them to south Wales, where he was endeavouring to raise new infantry levies to replace the troops lost at Naseby.

The immediate concern of the Parliamentarian Committee of Both Kingdoms was the large numbers of Royalist troops remaining in the west of England. If Charles followed the urgings of some of his advisers,and united his troops from south Wales with his Western armies, he might yet be able to bring numerically superior forces to bear against Sir Thomas Fairfax and the New Model and perhaps reverse the verdict of Naseby. For, though the Parliamentarians had suffered relatively light battle casualties, up to 4,000 foot may have deserted after the engagement, leaving Fairfax with no more than 13,000 men available for the next stage of the campaign.

The Council of War which Sir Thomas called after the recapture of Leicester (18 June) had two choices. One was to pursue the King into south Wales and disrupt his recruiting there. The alternative was to follow in the discouraging footsteps of the Earl of Essex twelve months earlier and march into the West. This option was given added force by concern for the garrison of Taunton. Its relief had been a major objective for Parliament throughout the spring and early summer. On 28 April the Committee of Both Kingdoms had ordered Fairfax to march to its aid. By 4 May Parliament's General had reached Salisbury, where he had initially ignored orders from the Committee to abandon his march in order to pursue the King. Only on 7 May, at Blandford, where he received an uncompromising repetition of his instructions, did Fairfax turn back eastwards, detaching a brigade of 4,000 men under Colonel Ralph Weldon to march on Taunton.

On Weldon's approach, the besiegers, under the temporary command of Lord Hopton and believing themselves to be faced by the whole of the New Model, pulled back to a strong defensive position in the Blagdon Hills. Weldon's orders were to resupply Taunton and then either re-join the New Model or link up with Parliament's Western Association forces under Edward Massey in the Gloucester area. On 28 May Goring made a bungled attempt to intercept and destroy Weldon at the start of his return march but, although the Parliamentarians escaped, they were forced to fall back into Taunton, where they remained for the duration of the siege.

As Fairfax and his commanders were aware, the Royalists promptly renewed their investment of Taunton, with an army 10,000 strong, under Goring's command. If Taunton fell, the Royalists would control the whole of the South-West, with the exceptions of Plymouth, Weymouth and Lyme. Sir Thomas referred the final decision to the Committee of Both Kingdoms and in the meantime marched to Marlborough in Wiltshire, from where he could implement either of his possible courses of action.

On 28 June he received the Committee's instructions. The Scots and local Parliamentarian forces were to deal with the King whilst Fairfax was to relieve Taunton and in the process defeat Goring and the last major Royalist field army. Two days later the Parliamentarians' march began.

Fairfax Moves West

The Royalists meanwhile were still attempting to agree on their post-Naseby strategy. Goring promised that, if he were permitted to press the siege, Taunton would fall within a few days, and so the King decided to continue his recruiting efforts in south Wales before ferrying his troops across the Bristol Channel and linking up with Goring. He was aware of the need for haste, writing on 1 July to Prince Rupert, currently organising the defences of Bristol:

> I desire your opinion how soon I shall pass the water, because all the forces which are already levied, I believe will be transported within five or six days, and it will be these ten days, at soonest, before the rest can be at the water-side. Now I would be loathe to stay for these last, because, before then it is likely there will be some action of moment.

It was indeed a closely matched race. If Fairfax did not move quickly, either Taunton might fall or he would face a combined army under Goring and the King superior in numbers to the New Model.

The Royalists' efforts, however, continued to be undermined by squabbling between the King's western commanders. Goring, despite his undoubted abilities, was notoriously and increasingly unreliable, and afflicted by both ill-health and the effects of drink. His operations against Taunton were in reality making little progress, whilst the depredations of his ill-disciplined troops alienated the local population, who often supported the armed neutralists known as 'Clubmen'.

Sir Thomas Fairfax (1612–71)

Fairfax had brief pre-Civil War military service abroad and in the First Scots War. In 1642 he became second in command to his father with the Parliamentarian forces based on the West Riding of Yorkshire. He proved an inspired leader in action if somewhat tongue-tied off the field. He had a series of successes, at Wakefield and Winceby in 1643 and at Nantwich in the following year. However, he had a tendency to rashness, exemplified in his comment at Winceby: 'Come, let us fall on. I never prospered better than when I fought against the enemy three or four to one.'

Fairfax was appointed to command the New Model Army largely as a compromise candidate acceptable to all political factions, but he proved his worth by his competent conduct of the Naseby campaign in 1645 and his assured command of the New Model thereafter.

Goring felt that he faced no immediate threat from the Parliamentarians. Their nearest troops — 2,000 horse of the Western Association under Edward Massey — were discounted by Goring as being too few to interfere with his operations, and he claimed that Taunton would fall before Fairfax could reach the area. However, by 24 June he had received word of Naseby and was changing his tune. He complained that, as a result of supply problems caused by the activities of the 'Clubmen' and the competing demands of the Royalist garrisons at Bristol and Langport, 'this army is almost as in great necessity of victuals as the Rebels at Taunton.' He claimed that, unless the situation improved in the next couple of days, he would be forced to raise the siege 'out of pure hunger'.

It may be that Goring was exaggerating his difficulties, for others placed the blame on the general himself. Clarendon, now serving with the Prince's Council, and admittedly a sworn enemy of Goring, wrote in late June: 'Lord Goring hath taken his pleasure of us, I pray God he doth not do so too of the King. . . . if he had been as much soldier as we expected that work had been done before this time, but he nothing but drinks and plays.'

Whilst there is little evidence to suggest that Goring's drinking had seriously impaired his military ability in the earlier part of his career, by the summer of 1645 it had become a serious problem. This was especially unfortunate because on occasion George Goring could still display flashes of his old brilliance. Richard Bulstrode, serving on Goring's staff that summer, recalled that his commander was

> . . . a Person of extraordinary abilities, as well as Courage, and was, without any Dispute, as good an Officer as any serving the King, and the most dextrous, in any sudden Emergency, that I have ever seen, and could extricate himself with the least Concern, of which I was a particular Eye-witness upon Several Occasions... But after all that can be said in General Goring's Behalf, he had likewise his blind Side, for he strangely loved the Bottle, was much given to his Pleasures and a great Debauchee, and the great Misfortune was, when he commanded in chief in the West of England, his Excellency had two Companions, who commanded next under him, who fed his wild Humour and Debauch, and one of them, if not both, wasted his great and natural Courage. These two Commanders, the one being Lieutenant-General, made the General turn his Wantoness into Riot, and his Riot into Madness. So that if the King had been truly informed of their continued strange Debauches, his Majesty would either have removed them from him, or all Three from future Trust or Employment . . .

The two confederates cited by Bulstrode were the Lieutenant General of Horse, Thomas, Lord Wentworth, who though personally brave was a notoriously poor disciplinarian, and Goring's Commissary General and brother-in-law, George Porter, who was both incompetent and quite possibly a coward.

Although it had been intended that Sir Richard Grenville should command the foot of the Western Army, Grenville remained unwilling to serve under Goring and had absented himself along with all but about 200 of his Cornish foot. For the present, Major General Sir Joseph Wagstaffe, who had commanded the Western Army foot under Prince Maurice, occupied the same post under Goring. Though rather sourly described by Clarendon as being given to 'jollity and mirth', Wagstaffe seems to have been a reasonably competent professional soldier.

By late June even Goring was forced to admit that there seemed to be no immediate prospect of capturing Taunton. His army had dwindled to about 3,000 horse and 4,000 foot, and the imminent prospect of intervention by the New Model forced the Royalists to reconsider their strategy. If faced by superior numbers, Goring proposed to reinforce the key Somerset garrisons of Bridgwater, Ilchester and Langport and pull the remainder of his troops back to defend the borders of Devon. However, Goring hoped to avoid such action by striking at Massey's brigade, currently at Dorchester, before it was reinforced by infantry from Poole. 'Having not a sufficient strength to take out as many as should oppose Massey and leave any of our quarters before Taunton secure but by lying there', Goring and his Council decided on 29 June to raise the siege and move to Chard, from where they hoped to engage Massey and his reinforcements before they could unite. Events were now moving rapidly.

On leaving Marlborough on 30 June the New Model Army totalled about 6,000 horse and 8,000 foot. Fairfax had good reason to be confident of the ability of his horse but his foot had not performed particularly well at Naseby and he may have been uneasy about some of them.

Lieutenant General and second in command of the New Model was Oliver Cromwell. Although not yet looming as large in contemporary eyes as he would to posterity, Cromwell had already made his mark as an outstanding cavalry commander, having played a major role in the victories at Marston Moor and Naseby as well as having a number of lesser successes to his credit. The old warhorse Philip Skippon, who had been appointed Major General of Foot to the New Model, was still out of action as a result of the wounds he suffered at Naseby. Colonel Robert Hammond was probably deputising for him. The New Model had an effective artillery train, including two brass demi-culverins and eight sakers, supplemented by a number of Royalist guns captured at Naseby.

Fairfax knew that he would have to move rapidly if he were to deal with Goring before the latter was reinforced from south Wales. To avoid delay, he decided against taking the most direct route towards Taunton, which would risk interference from the Royalist forces at Bristol, and instead follow a more southerly line, which would also enable him to be supplied by sea through the Parliamentarian-held coastal towns.

Despite scorchingly hot weather and the stifling clouds of dust on the roads, the New Model moved fast. On the first day of their march they covered a remarkable thirty miles. During the night of 30 June they halted at Amesbury, and next day pressed on to Salisbury. Averaging about fourteen miles a day, Fairfax linked up with Massey on 4 June at Beauminster, about seven miles south of Crewkerne. Patrols brought in some Royalist prisoners, who confirmed that Goring had raised the siege of Taunton and was now at Ilminster, reportedly en route to Somerton.

Langport: The Campaign

Crewkerne was a strategically important road centre, with links to the main towns of the area. The marshy nature of the terrain, traversed by the Rivers Parrot, Isle and Yeo and numerous tributary streams, meant that the Parliamentary advance would be confined to the roads, the river lines and bridges affording good advantages for defence.

Oliver Cromwell (1598–1658)

A Huntingdonshire country gentleman with no prewar military experience, Cromwell in 1642 was best known for his political opposition to the King. 'His stature was of a good size, his countenance swollen and reddish, his voice sharp and untenable, and his eloquence full of fervor.'

In the opening months of the war Cromwell threw himself into military affairs in Parliament's Eastern Association, and in a number of actions during 1643 — at Grantham, Gainsborough and Winceby — proved to be an excellent cavalry commander. His prominent role at Marston Moor set Cromwell on the road to military fame, and his influence among the Independent faction in Parliament assured him of the post of Lieutenant General of Horse in the New Model Army — a choice the wisdom of which was confirmed at Naseby.

Edward Hyde, 1st Earl of Clarendon (1609–74). Chancellor of the Exchequer and a close adviser to Charles I, Hyde accompanied the Prince of Wales to the West in 1645. His History of the Great Rebellion *is a major contemporary source for the Civil War.*

Goring had indeed now received orders from the King to stand on the defensive until he was reinforced from south Wales, and by Grenville and Berkley moving up from the West. In reality, outnumbered by at least two to one, Goring had little option. He could only hope to delay Fairfax by making maximum use of the terrain in the vicinity of Langport, which consisted of enclosed countryside crossed by narrow, steeply banked lanes and with a number of rivers forming natural barriers.

His hope was to hold the line of the River Yeo from its junction with the River Parrett south-eastwards towards Ilchester, and so protect the vital supply base of Bridgwater and the north Somerset ports on the Bristol Channel, through which the first of the troops from south Wales had begun to arrive. At least two regiments, totalling about 1,500 men, landed at the beginning of July at Uphill, and more were expected. A Parliamentarian newspaper admitted: 'this is our problem still, Bristol for ammunition, Wales for men.'

Fairfax's troops were beginning to feel the effects of their long marches when, on 5 July, the New Model resumed its advance in 'a very hot season, the foot weary with the long and tedious march; the carriage horses tired out, the way ill and narrow.' Colonel Charles Fleetwood, with 2,000 horse and dragoons, was sent to push back a Royalist outpost at Petherton on the River Parrett and secure and repair the bridge there. The Royalists fell back on Ilchester, and Edward Montagu's brigade of foot was sent to support Fleetwood and secure the crossing at South Marlock.

Partly because it was the Sabbath, and also because his exhausted men and horses needed rest, Fairfax halted on 6 July and did not resume operations until the following day. The pause allowed the less religious — or more desperate — Royalists time to break down all of the bridges over the River Yeo apart from the strongly defended structures at Long Load and Ilchester. Throughout 7 July skirmishing continued between parties of horse in the meadows around Ilchester whilst Fairfax and his commanders considered their next move. The Parliamentarians had two unattractive alternatives. They could either make a lengthy march north-westwards to the head of the Yeo or they could attempt to force a crossing of the river at some nearer point. Their Council of War decided on the latter course and resolved to make their attack at Yeovil, about five miles south-east of Ilchester.

Neither course was particularly inviting, but the Parliamentarians now had a stroke of luck. Goring apparently assumed that the Yeovil crossing would be defended by Sir Lewis Dyve, Governor of nearby Sherbourne Castle, but, owing to some confusion, the crossing was left unguarded and the Parliamentarians were able to occupy it without opposition and outflank the line of the Yeo.

When news of this reached Goring at his headquarters at Long Sutton he ordered the outposts at Long Load and Ilchester to be abandoned and fell back on Langport. He still hoped to delay Fairfax, or at any rate to lessen the odds against him, by causing the Parliamentarian commander to divide his forces, and on 8 July, with this in mind, he sent George Porter with his own, Wentworth's and Sir Edward Stawell's brigades of horse — 1,500 men in all — in a feint in the direction of Taunton.

Fairfax reacted as had been hoped, sending Massey and his Western Brigade — about 3,000 horse — in pursuit. However, Goring had erred in his choice of commander. Speed and alertness were essential but, perhaps because of the continuing hot weather, Porter fatally dawdled. At noon on 9 July his men were quietly relaxing on the banks of the River Isle at Isle Abbot. They had, it is true, placed a small garrison in the church, together with a few dragoons at the entrance to the village, but had taken few other precautions, evidently unaware of the proximity of the enemy. Massey was not a man to waste such an opportunity. He

> . . . drew his men into two divisions, for each end of the town one, himself commanded one, and Captain Gutteridge the other, which was but a small party, for Colonel Massey commanded the main body himself. Massey's men marched with green boughs in their hats. Gutteridge coming in the town's end, found the hedges lined with Musketeers at the southwest end of the town. Captain Fransway, a Dutch Captain, commanded a party to fall on the

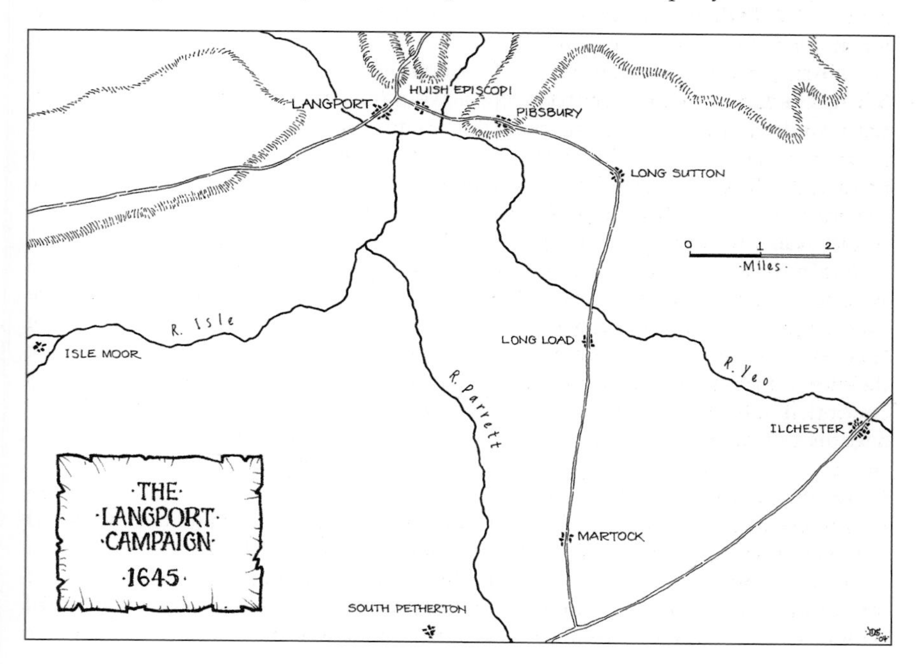

Oliver Cromwell (1599–1658).

one side of the ambushers, and Captain Gutteridge on the other. The Dutch Captain when he was charged by the enemy, began to face about, which impeded Captain Gutteridge's prosecution of the business, yet the rest of the officers and soldiers, with the wisdom of Captain Gutteridge, ended the business so well that they beat up their ambuscades for all that, and drove them quite away: in the meantime Major General Massey marched up to the other side of the town, and Colonel Massey with Colonel Cooke and the rest, raised them, and those with the rest at the other end of the town, followed so hard upon the enemy, that they drove them all from the town, pursuing them within two miles of Langport.

News of the encounter reached Goring and he hurried to the scene, just in time to see Porter in full flight at the head of the fugitives. With the enraged comment that his brother-in-law 'deserves to be pistolled for his Negligence and Cowardice', Goring flung himself into the fray. He was wounded, nearly having an ear severed, but rallied his troopers and checked the enemy pursuit 'and made a handsome retreat, without which the best part of the Army would have been lost that day.' As it was, the damage was serious enough. Porter had lost about thirty dead, 200 prisoners, 250 horses and nine colours, and Goring's slim remaining chance of holding the line of the Yeo was at an end.

Whilst the action had been taking place at Isle Abbot, skirmishing had also been in progress between Fairfax's main force and the remainder of Goring's horse to the east of Langport. Fairfax seems to have had the best of the fighting, taking some prisoners, including a French cornet, a Dutchman and a Spaniard. However, during the afternoon, hearing 'the muskets go off very thick towards Major General Massey's quarters' and believing him to be under attack, Fairfax detached Edward Montagu's Regiment of Foot to his assistance.

Langport: The Battle

These were a few less opponents for Goring to face, but his plans had been wrecked by Porter's negligence. Not only had the Royalist position on the Yeo been rendered untenable, there was also a danger that Massey might force a crossing of the river at Barrow and threaten Goring's rear. Few options were available to the Royalist Council of War when it met that evening, for, as Goring later admitted:

> . . . we could not disengage ourselves from the Rebels without the certain loss of our Cannon and hazard of the Army if we had retreated that night, the Enemy having come very close about us on every side, our horse having been very much shattered with the disorder that day, the way not being passible [*sic*] for our Cannon on that side and there being not one day's provision in Langport.

The Royalists decided on the risky but unavoidable course of attempting a phased withdrawal, probably under enemy attack, to the strongly fortified garrison of Bridgwater, from where they could still hope to link up with reinforcements from south Wales. First they would send off the bulk of their guns and foot whilst a rearguard, including most of the horse, would fight a delaying action by holding a strong position just to the east of Langport.

The Parliamentarians, meanwhile, were increasingly worried. As Cromwell explained:

> We were advanced to Long Sutton, near a very strong place of the Enemy's, called Langport; far from our Garrisons, without much ammunition, in a place extremely wanting in provisions, - the Malignant Clubmen interposing, who are ready to take all advantages against our parties, and would undoubtedly take them against our Army, if they had opportunity. — Goring stood upon the advantage of strong passes, staying until the rest of his recruits came up to his Army, with a resolution not to engage until Grenville and Prince Charles his men were come up to him. We could not well have necessitated him to an Engagement, nor have stayed one day longer without retreating to our ammunition and to conveniency [*sic*] of victual.'

So, on the morning of 10 July, the Parliamentarian commanders were debating the prospect of retreating towards Sherbourne and Yeovil in order to rest their men and pick up supplies brought by sea — and, in effect, giving Goring the time to gain reinforcements which he had been fighting for. Then, in Cromwell's description, 'word was brought us, that the Enemy drew out. He did so, with a resolution to send most of his cannon and baggage to Bridgewater [*sic*] — which he effected —but with a resolution not to fight, but, trusting to his ground, thinking he could make away at pleasure.'

Edward Massey (?1619–?1674). A professional soldier, Massey came to prominence after his successful defence of Gloucester in 1643. In 1645, as General of the Western Association, he co-operated with Fairfax and the New Model.

The Royalist position viewed from the eastern side of the Wagg Rhyne.

Fairfax and his senior commanders rode out to inspect Goring's position, and without any formal resolution by a council of war 'the Army was ordered to be put in Battalia', and orders sent for Montagu's foot to return from Massey. However, before they could arrive, fighting had begun.

Fairfax was probably on the move at the first glimmer of light, about 3 a.m., when his men began to deploy in Sutton Field. The troops available totalled about 10,000 men, 2,000 of them horse. A considerable number of Fairfax's best troops were still with Massey, about twelve miles away and separated from Fairfax by three rivers. With Sir Thomas were six regiments of horse, under Cromwell, consisting of Fairfax's, Whalley's, Cromwell's, Rich's, Fleetwood's and Butler's units, and the complete foot regiments of Welden, Herbert, Ingoldsby, Fortescue, Skippon, Russell, Hammond, Rainsborough and Sir Hardrass Waller together with the pikes of Fairfax, Montagu and Pickering's regiments.

Even as the New Model began to deploy, Goring and the bulk of his army took up position on Ham Down, a ridge varying between 80 and 100 feet in height and situated a mile north-east of Langport. The Royalists were strongly posted. Between the ridges — mainly enclosed ground which had formerly been the open field system of Pibsbury, Pitnet and Huish Episcopi and where the two armies were now deploying — a stream, the Wagg Rhyne, ran south-westwards through the shallow valley to join the River Yeo. Recent heavy rain — possibly a thunderstorm following the hot weather —had swollen the normally shallow stream so that it could only be crossed via a ford about 50 yards south of the modern Wagg Bridge. On the Langport side of the ford the now muddy lane ran uphill to Ham Down. It was only wide enough for four horsemen to ride abreast and was lined on either side by thick hedges, with small hedged enclosures on either hand. The right (southern) flank of the Royalist position was protected by the River Yeo, whilst any attempt to outflank it from the north would give the Royalists time to complete their objective of withdrawing to Bridgwater.

Goring had lined the hedges along the lane and its surrounding fields with about 2,000 musketeers, mainly from the recently arrived south Wales foot regiments of Matthew Wise and John Slaughter. Two field guns were positioned covering the ford whilst the horse were drawn up to the rear on Ham Down. The first division, deployed close to where the lane opened out on to the Down, apparently consisted mainly of the once excellent brigade of horse from the Oxford Army which had been commanded in 1644 by the Earl of Cleveland. It included his own Regiment, now led by Colonel Sir Arthur Slingsby, Lord Goring's Regiment, commanded by his brother, Lieutenant Colonel Charles Goring, and Lord Goring's Lifeguard under Colonel Patrick Barnwell. Goring himself was with this body, which probably totalled about 800 men.

It is unclear how much of the Royalist army was still with Goring: the heavy artillery was already on the road to Bridgwater. The bulk of the foot, under Major-General Sir Joseph Wagstaffe, were drawn up to the right of Goring, with orders to retreat through Langport for Bridgewater if the Parliamentarians gained the upper hand. They may already have been in process of following the artillery. However, Goring still had about 2,500 horse and the 2,000 musketeers. There could be no certainty as to how well these troops would fight. Many of the foot were new recruits, and the morale and degree of commitment of the veteran horse was now doubtful. Goring had to hope that advantages of terrain would help to offset these deficiencies, at least long enough to allow his foot and guns to get clear.

Goring's Brigade Major, Sir Richard Bulstrode, later described his commander's plan:

> After the beating up of Lieutenant General Porter's Quarters, Fairfax, with his Army, marched directly on us from Yeovil, where, being in a plain and rising Ground, the Enemy's Army was drawn up upon it, with a great Marsh and Bogg between both Armies, which hindered the Enemy from attacking up, except by one Passage in the Bottom of the Hill, between both Armies, which Passage was narrow, and our General had placed there two Regiments of foot

Looking eastwards across the fields occupied by Royalist musketeers.

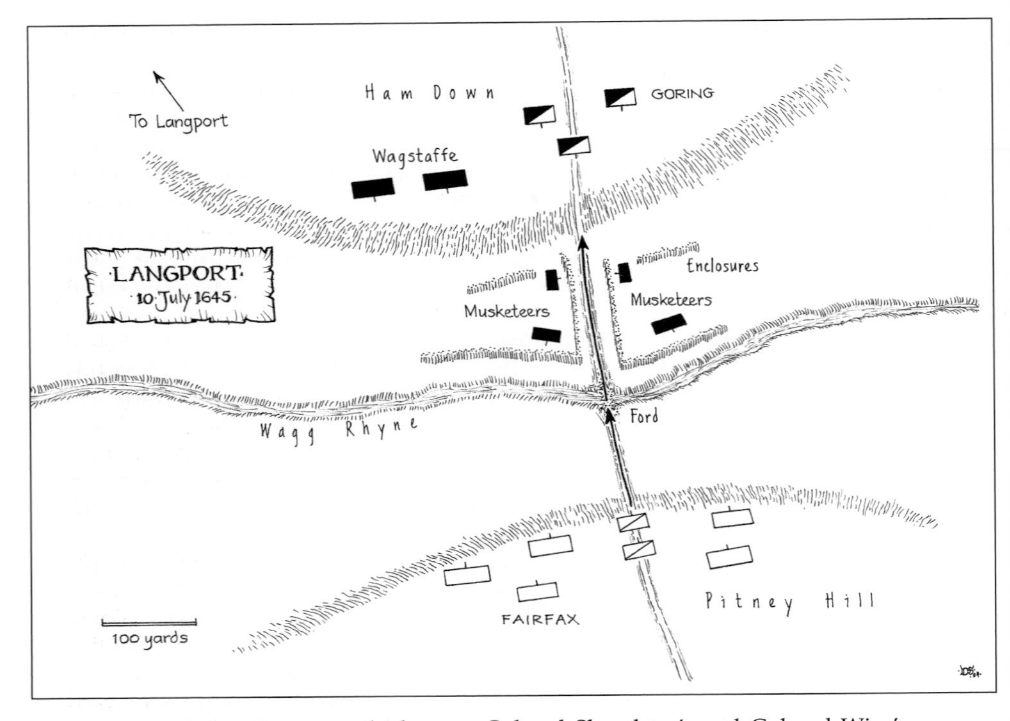

to guard that Passage; which were Colonel Slaughter's and Colonel Wise's Regiments, lately raised in south Wales. General Goring himself, with all his Horse, was drawn up upon the Hill, at the mouth of the Passage, with the infantry upon his right Hand, near Langport, to succour those two Regiments, in case of attack upon the Pass, which the General hoped to make good, at least till Night, that then we might retire with less Loss, being unseen. In the meantime, General Goring commanded me to send away all the Baggage and Cannon, except two Field Pieces, which he commanded should be drawn to the top of the Hill, at the Head of the Pass, and bid me to order Sir Joseph Wagstaffe from him, who commanded the Foot near to Langport, that in case the Enemy should force the Pass upon him, that then Sir Joseph Wagstaffe should retire with all his Foot to Langport, and there pass the River towards Bridgewater [*sic*] and burn down the Bridge behind him, which was a Draw-bridge over the River; and in the Morning, when I had Orders to send away the baggage and Cannon, I sent them that Way, for their greater Security, otherwise they had been all lost . . .

Fairfax also had reasons for concern. The performance of many of the New Model foot at Naseby had done little to inspire confidence, especially as they might now be required to force a strong defensive position. As a Parliamentarian writer admitted, 'the passage to them was extreme dangerous, being so straight, that four horse could hardly pass abreast, and that up to the belly in water, they lying so in flanks and front to receive us.' It may be because of this uncertainty that, although both sides were in position at least by 7 a.m., a lull followed for the next five hours, and it was not until scouts and local sympathisers confirmed to Fairfax that Goring was withdrawing his guns and foot that the Parliamentarian commanders, meeting near a windmill on Somerton Hill, agreed that they would have to move quickly if Goring were not to achieve his aim. Whilst they were still debating, 'it pleased God to end the businesse by an Alarm given us, that the Enemy had possessed the Passe we formerly skirmished at in Pissebury-Bottom, and some of their Foot appeared on the Hill; whereupon the Forces we had on this side the River [Yeo] were drawn forth.'

Fairfax had positioned his lighter guns on the ridge, Pitney Hill, which ran parallel to the Wagg Rhyne, about 700 yards from the main Royalist position. They opened up in a bombardment lasting for about half an hour, 'the cannon playing their part as gallantly as ever I saw gunners in my life,' as one Parliamentarian eyewitness remarked. Although Goring's two guns replied, the encounter was largely one-sided. After fifty or sixty shots had been directed at them, the outmatched Royalist pieces were silenced and Goring's musketeers sufficiently disordered for Fairfax to launch the next phase of his attack.

About 1,500 'commanded' musketeers under Colonel Thomas Rainsborough, seconded by Weldon's Regiment, advanced and began a firefight with the Royalist musketeers along the valley bottom. The resistance was patchy. Bulstrode claimed that some of the Welsh foot behaved badly, even firing on their own troops, but this is not confirmed by other sources. However, it seems that a number of Wise's and Slaughter's men were pressed Parliamentarian prisoners, and they may have seized the opportunity to defect.

According to Bulstrode, Goring, watching the opening of the engagement from Ham Down, was unpleasantly surprised by the size of the enemy force confronting him:

The high ground on which the Parliamentarians deployed, viewed from Ham Down.

> Yet so soon as the Enemy had put their Army in Order of Battle, upon the Top of the Hill, on the other Side the Bogg, which we thought was their whole Army, they opened and drew to their Right and Left, advancing towards the Pass, whilst another great Body came up in their Place, by which their Army was more than double our Number.

Soon after noon Rainsborough's men began to push across the Wagg Rhyne and, the ford partially secured, it was time for the next stage of Fairfax's plan. Consulting with Cromwell, and realising that speed and a shock attack were vital, Sir Thomas decided upon a bold stroke. Cromwell 'commanded Major Bethel to charge them with two Troops of about one hundred and twenty horse'. Other accounts suggest that Major Christopher Bethell actually led forward three troops of Edward Whalley's Horse (part of Cromwell's old regiment), supported by three troops of Fairfax's Regiment under Major Desborough, with orders to charge straight up the lane through the fire of the remaining Royalist musketeers and into the ranks of Goring's horse. It was a calculated gamble, in some ways uncomfortably reminiscent of a similar action by Fairfax at Marston Moor that had resulted in disaster, but the Parliamentarian commanders had confidence in the training and morale of their splendid horse and the Royalists' resistance was clearly faltering. In any case, they had little option.

Bethell and his troopers splashed across the ford, galloped full tilt up the lane, shrugging off the ragged fire of the remaining enemy musketeers, and reached the point where the road debouched on to Ham Down. Their impetus carried them into the front ranks of Goring's division of horse and a hand-to-hand fight continued 'whilst you could count three or four hundred'. Bethell's leading troop forced back Goring's first division by the impetus of its attack and provided space for his other two troops to begin deploying at the head of the lane. They broke a second division

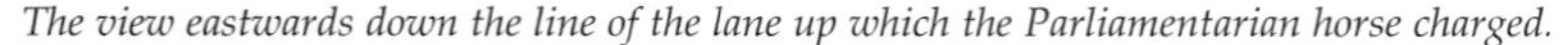

The view eastwards down the line of the lane up which the Parliamentarian horse charged.

The view of the lane from the Parliamentarian side. Note the hedges on either side.

of 400 Royalist horse, but Goring now personally led a counter-charge and Bethell, 'somewhat overborne at last', recoiled towards Desborough's men, who were by now also deploying at the head of the lane, about 300 yards behind. Lieutenant-Colonel Lilburne related how

> . . . it coming to Major Bethell's turne to charge with his forlorne of horse, which consisted of 3 Troopes of Col. Wales [Whalley's] Regiment, viz Major Bethell's, Captaine Evinson's and Capt. Groves: Major Desborowe with 3 Troops of the Generalls owne Regiment being to second them, Bethell upon command given, led on his own troop through the water which was deepe and dirty and very narrow, the Enemy having a very large body at the top of the lane, many times over his number, charged them with as much gallantry as ever I saw men in my life, forcing them with the sword to give ground, which made way for Capt Evinson's Troope to draw out of the lane, and front with him, driving the enemies great body and their reserve up the hill, but a very great fresh body of the Enemies horse coming upon them, forced them to retreat to Capt. Grove who was their reserve, who drawing his men close, received the enemy with much bravery and resolution, and gave liberty to his friends to rally and front with him who all three charged the enemies numerous bodies very furiously and routed them quite, which made way for our musketeers to run up the hedges and gall the enemy, and for Major Desborowe [*sic*] to draw his 3 Troops out of the lane and front with Bethell.

Desborough 'with the General's Troop sheltered him [Bethell] by his flank to rally, and charged up himself with about 200 horse of the General's Regiment.' This part of Fairfax's Regiment seems to have fallen on the open left flank of Goring's horse, and Royalist resistance speedily collapsed. Goring may have attempted to lead another unsuccessful counter-attack but admitted that his troopers 'only made one seasonable charge'; indeed, Desborough's attack was enough to 'set them all a-running, gained freedom by it for all our horse and foot, to draw into bodies, sent the enemy running, not being able to endure another charge.'

Fairfax and Cromwell, watching from their command post on Pibsbury Down, commended Bethell and Desborough's charge 'for the most gallant piece of service that ever was in England'. The two majors continued to demonstrate the superior discipline and control that was the hallmark of the New Model horse by halting and re-forming their men until reinforcements came up 'that the pursuit might be orderly, and with good reserves, in case the enemy should face about and charge again.'

There was little prospect of this. Most of the Welsh musketeers had by now been ridden down, been captured or switched sides, whilst Goring's horse were in full flight. Some of them became bogged down in the numerous watercourses and, abandoning their horses, made off on foot.

Some of the fleeing Royalist foot set fire to houses in Langport in an attempt to delay pursuit, but Cromwell urged the New Model horse on through the burning street. He caught up with some of the retreating Royalists two or three miles beyond the town and rounded up two or three hundred prisoners. Goring unsuccessfully attempted to organise a stand at the village of Aller and then, accompanied by his staff and such of his Lifeguard as he could rally, headed for Bridgwater.

Arriving there, Goring was 'overjoyed' to find that Wagstaffe had already arrived with most of the guns and foot. Two days later, writing to Lord Digby, Goring attempted to minimise the extent of his defeat:

> . . . our foot got into Langport which way my Lord Wentworth retired with some of our horse and he and Sir Joseph Wagstaffe brought off all our foot to Bridgewater [*sic*] (there was only two pieces of cannon lost, the rest to Bridgewater and left there) without the loss of two hundred. The rest of our horse went another way towards Bridgewater and could never be brought to rally but in small and disorderly bodies. Our losses was not great for we are told by one of the Enemy there were not 300 prisoners and I am confident we had not twenty men killed.

Goring's view was, to say the least, optimistic. The Parliamentarians claimed to have killed 300 of the enemy and taken over 2,000 prisoners, together with 2,100 horses, thirty colours and two guns. Most of the 2,000 musketeers — about half of Goring's total number of foot — will have made up the bulk of the prisoners. The Parliamentarians admitted to 'not twenty' dead, though fourteen or fifteen of Bethell's Troop were wounded and their commander had been shot in the hand.

Whatever gloss Goring might attempt to put on its outcome, Langport was a crushing blow to remaining Royalist hopes. Admitting that 'there is so great a terror and distraction amongst our men that I am confident at the present they could not be brought to fight against half their number', and with his foot deserting or falling victim to vengeful Clubmen, Goring strengthened his remaining garrisons, left his guns in Bridgwater and withdrew into Devon.

Fairfax recognised the importance of his victory. As he explained to his father,

> It pleased God to give them this blow in good season. The King had given Goring strict command not to engage before himself, with the Welsh forces, and Grenville with those out of the West[arrived] which, altogether, would have been a very great army, so as we cannot esteem this mercy less, all things considered, than that of Naseby fight.

News of the defeat at Langport caused King Charles to abandon his plans to join his forces in the West. Fairfax, with no effective Royalist force left to oppose him in the field, was free to turn his attention to the enemy garrisons. His first target was the great Royalist supply depot of Bridgwater, which was stormed on 23 July and yielded a rich haul in guns and other munitions.

Autumn Campaign

Goring could have done little to prevent Fairfax from driving on deep into the West, but he gained a temporary respite when the New Model turned back eastwards towards the rich prize of Bristol, which, with other garrisons, Fairfax was unwilling to leave in Royalist hands threatening his communications. Bath was occupied on 30 July and Sherbourne Castle fell on 14 August, and on 10 September, recognising the futility of further resistance when his outer defences were stormed, Prince Rupert surrendered Bristol — and was disgraced as a result.

Leaving Cromwell to mop up the Royalist garrisons in Wiltshire and Hampshire, Fairfax turned his attention back to the West. The Royalists still controlled all of Cornwall and much of Devon, with the exception of Plymouth. They had, however, made little use of their breathing space in which to address their problems. The Prince of Wales' Council of the West continued, theoretically, to exercise overall authority, but the lack of any clear command structure and control over the various quarrelling generals continued to cripple its efforts. What discipline remained after Langport in Goring's beaten army was rapidly dissolving as his cavalry made unreasonable demands for contributions from the civilian population of north Devon, where they were quartered, as well as openly plundering. Goring still had about 2,500 horse and 3,000–4,000 foot under his command, and although he was increasingly sinking into drunken debauchery he would in any case have had severe problems in maintaining his army. He was crippled by lack of funds, informing the Council on 18 July that 'I have a great desire to reform both [horse and foot] but it cannot be done without some pay to them.'

Goring's army was shifted to south Devon, in order to cover the approaches to Exeter, where their depredations quickly resumed, whilst Goring fell into dispute with the Governor of Exeter, Sir John Berkeley. Moreover, time was now running out: by early October Fairfax was ready to turn his attention back to the West.

On 14 October the New Model occupied Honiton in Devon. Fairfax was once again acting on the instructions of the Committee of Both Kingdoms, which was anxious about the safety of Plymouth, under loose Royalist blockade. Although, on paper, the Royalists still possessed significant forces in the West, they were in no state to present any co-ordinated opposition to Fairfax's advance. Goring continued to hover indecisively around Exeter, sending part of his cavalry under Lord Wentworth to link up with Grenville's Cornish troops at Okehampton. On 15 October

Charles, Prince of Wales (1630–85). A youth aged fifteen, Charles was sent to the West by the King both to gain experience and to be safer from possible capture. By the closing stages of the war he was taking an increasing part in decision-making.

Fairfax reached Cullompton and on the 18th Crediton, and on the 19th the Parliamentarians surprised and captured Tiverton Castle.

Assured that Plymouth was in no immediate danger, the Parliamentarian commanders decided to make Exeter their principal objective. They were unwilling to risk suffering Essex's fate by making any major advance into Cornwall with the principal remaining Royalist garrison in the West still unsubdued in their rear, and it was in any case late in the year to undertake prolonged field operations.

Setting up a series of outposts to form a loose blockade around Exeter, Fairfax withdrew the bulk of his forces into winter quarters around Ottery St Mary and spent the next few weeks steadily tightening his grip on the Royalists' western capital. Goring, claiming that active operations were at an end for the year, seized the excuse to depart for France on grounds of health, falsely promising that he would return in the spring.

Goring's departure had little practical effect. He had handed over command of his troops to Lord Wentworth, who was equally unable to control them. Sir Richard Grenville meanwhile withdrew his Cornish forces to the line of the River Tamar and, in a move which might either denote a form of Cornish separatism or presage an attempt to take control on his own account, gave orders that attempts by Wentworth's men to enter Cornwall were to be resisted, describing them as 'unruly troopers as do plunder and abuse the country'. His own proposals to the Prince of Wales involved attempting to reach a separate peace with Parliament, under which Cornwall, and part of Devon, would be allowed an autonomous position under the Prince. Needless to say, there was not the slightest possibility of either Prince Charles or Parliament agreeing to this.

The Royalists had been given some slight encouragement by widespread sickness among the Parliamentarian troops, and, hoping to take advantage of this, on 27 December the Prince moved his headquarters east from Truro to Tavistock with a view to organising a counter-attack. He announced that 'Whereas upon the motion of the enemy on this side Exeter, we have resolved in our own person to repair to our Army and to . . . advance with our forces hoping by the blessing of God to repel the enemy from this county.' His plan was to call out the Devon *posse comitatus*, together with the county Trained Bands, then, using Totnes as his base, advance through south Devon on Exeter. At the same time a force under Major-General Guy Molesworth, consisting of 800 foot and a brigade of horse, was to advance from Okehampton. If Wentworth co-operated, the Prince hoped to have about 5,000 horse and 6,000 foot available, numerically equal to the New Model if greatly inferior in quality.

Fairfax, getting wind of Royalist plans, struck first. On 9 January 1646, in a pre-emptive strike, Parliamentarian horse led by Oliver Cromwell beat up Wentworth's quarters at Bovey Tracy. Some 400 horses and some prisoners were taken, although Wentworth and his principal officers escaped from their billet by the expedient of throwing £10 in coins out of the window and making off whilst Cromwell's troopers were scrabbling for them. At the same time other Parliamentarian troops beat up Royalist quarters at Ashburton and Totnes. The final blow to the Prince's plan came on 18 January, when, after consolidating his hold on south Devon, Fairfax stormed the port of Dartmouth. Apart from depriving the Royalists of one of their few remaining ports, the fall of Dartmouth meant that they could no longer maintain the blockade of Plymouth.

Hopton Takes Command

Faced with imminent defeat, the Prince and his Council decided on a last desperate gamble. It was on 16 January that Sir Richard Grenville had written to the Prince urging that he appoint a commander-in-chief for his remaining forces. Ruling himself out on health grounds — perhaps not entirely sincerely — Grenville had proposed either the Earl of Forth or Lord Hopton. Charles had already made such a request to Hopton on the previous day.

Ralph Hopton was both older and in poorer health than in the days in the spring of 1643 when he had been seen as the saviour of the Royalist cause in the West. Although he accepted the command, he had few illusions, telling the Prince that

> It was a custom now, when men were not willing to submit to what they were enjoined, to say that it was against their honour; that their honour would not suffer them to do this or that: for his part he could not obey his highness at this time without resolving to lose his honour, which he knew he must, but since his highness thought it necessary to command him, he was ready to obey him with loss of honour.

As he took command of what Clarendon accurately termed 'a dissolute, indisciplined, wicked, beaten army upon which he must engage his honour . . . without any time to reform or instruct', Hopton had few expectations of ultimate victory. His mood was expressed by the fatalistic motto on his personal standard for the coming campaign: 'I will Strive to Serve My Sovereign King'.

Hopton's command got off to an inauspicious start. Although Lord Wentworth agreed to serve as Lieutenant General of Horse, Sir Richard Grenville, in a *volte face*, declined to be Major General of Foot, demanding instead the responsibility for maintaining security in Cornwall and rounding up deserters. Though he had considerable proven talents for this role, the Prince and his Council suspected

Grenville of treacherous intent and on 18 January he was arrested and confined to St Michael's Mount. His replacement, Major General Robert Harris, was not the man to reconcile Grenville's disgruntled Cornishmen, who rapidly lost interest in continuing the fight.

According to Hopton's own account, the troops under his command were from a wide mixture of units. The bulk of the horse consisted of the 2,500 survivors of Goring's forces, led by Lord Wentworth. They included the remnants of several formerly well-respected regiments from the Oxford Army. However, defeat and sagging morale and discipline had played havoc with these men and Hopton had little respect for them. Though they included a number of gallant officers, they were 'never able to surprise or attempt upon the enemy, but ever liable to be surprised by them: and of this I often told the General Officers, but could not in that short time better regulate it . . .' They proved to be largely useless for reconnaissance and guard duties, and they 'never kept their hour upon rendezvous in any tolerable proportion, nor sent their numbers commanded to the guards, nor for the most part stayed with their officers upon duty . . . I do not remember any one guard that ever I justified, while I had to do with them.'

The best cavalry available to Hopton were Prince Charles' Regiment, an amalgamation of several units, 800 strong, commanded by Arthur, Lord Capel. Hopton described them as 'a very handsome body of men, and very exact upon duty'. Unfortunately, they did not compensate for the deficiencies of the remainder of the horse and, inexplicably (though allegedly on the grounds of shortage of fodder), Hopton chose not to take them with him on his final campaign.

The Royalist foot were also a mixed bunch. Once again, the best of them seem to have been the 250 men of the Prince of Wales's Regiment (formerly Sir John Acland's) which had been raised from West Country tin miners. The remainder, totalling in theory about 3,000 men though in practice probably fewer after the defection of some of Grenville's Cornish, were of very variable quality.

It was with this generally unpromising material that Hopton prepared to attempt to restore the Royalists' fortunes in the West. His most urgent task was the relief of Exeter, whose citizens were becoming increasingly restive as the effects of the Parliamentarian blockade began to bite. If this could somehow be achieved, there then appears to have been a rather vague plan to unite with the surviving Royalist horse based on Oxford.

Arthur, Lord Capel (1610–49). After an unsuccessful period in command of Royalist forces in the Welsh Marches, Capel took over the Prince of Wales's Lifeguard for the last campaign in the West.

A Royalist soldier in the later stages of the war. The Montero cap seen here was a popular item of headgear, particularly, it seems, among Royalist troops.

Hopton mustered his army at Launceston, from where it would march to Torrington in north Devon. Here it would be reinforced from the Royalist garrison at Barnstaple before marching southwards via Chudleigh towards Exeter. For the moment the Parliamentarians were still fairly widely scattered in their quarters. On 26 January Sir Thomas Fairfax was at Powderham Castle, infantry under Sir Hardrass Waller and Richard Ingoldsby at Crediton and Chudleigh and other units near Exeter, at Dartmouth and at Totnes. The bulk of the disorderly Royalist cavalry were still around Holsworthy in north Devon, where they were noted as being 'only terrible in plunder and resolute in running away . . . whom only their friends feared and their enemies laughed at.'

Fairfax now held a Council of War at Totnes and, in the absence of any clear indications of the enemy's movement, decided to resume close operations against Exeter. He moved his own headquarters to Chudleigh and on 27 January sent Sir John Berkeley at Exeter a summons to surrender, which was rejected.

By now, however, there were indications that Hopton was planning a move. Reports reached Fairfax on 3 February that 'Divers horses, all laden, some with provisions have been sent out of Launceston westward. There was also great store of bread baked.' Other materials being gathered included 'muskets, pikes and other ammunition, the rest of loading was victuals as powdered Beef or Cheese, with them were about four horses laden with powder, match and Bullets and Lead.' However, Fairfax's spy told him that 'the Cornish remain adverse to any march or service and though they come in to avoid displeasure yet they make away again' others were said to have been pressed by force, or brought along tied up.

Hopton's main problem was the slow arrival at Launceston of his supplies. On 8 February, deciding that he could afford to wait no longer, the Royalist commander marched via Stratton to Torrington, where he arrived on 9 February and, with only half of his promised supplies yet with him, called a halt to wait for the rest to come up.

On 8 February Fairfax had summoned a Council of War at Crediton to consider his response to the reports from Launceston. He had already been thinking of moving into north Devon in order to ease the supply situation for his forces around Exeter and to drive out the Royalist cavalry quartered there. Whilst the Council was still deliberating, news arrived that Hopton was on the march and would arrive at

Torrington in two days' time, having told Sir John Berkeley that relief was on the way. Fairfax called a general rendezvous for the next day and planned his counter moves.

The blockade of Exeter was to be maintained by Sir Hardrass Waller with three regiments each of horse and foot whilst the remainder of the New Model was concentrated against Hopton. For four days, until 13 February, Fairfax remained at Crediton, hoping to be reinforced by additional troops under Phillip Skippon, but by the 14th, unable to wait any longer, he decided to press on with the troops available. The Parliamentarian force consisted of Fairfax's, Hammond's, Harlow's, Lambert's, Fortescue's and Ingoldsby's Regiments of Foot and Cromwell's, Pye's and Rich's Regiments of Horse, together with five troops of dragoons under Captain Wogan — in all, about 4,000 foot, 1,500 horse and 500 dragoons.

The Battle of Torrington

On 14 February Fairfax advanced about ten miles to Chimleigh, 'the weather wet, and the way very dirty', where he received news that the Royalists were still at Torrington. The Parliamentarians rendezvoused next morning, intending to have resumed their advance, but it became obvious that they were so much hindered by bad weather and broken-down bridges that Fairfax abandoned the march for the day after a brief attempt and returned to Chimleigh with his main body. He sent a party consisting of his own Regiment of Foot and 200 horse under Captain Berry in the direction of Ash Reirney 'to amuse the enemy'. At Burrington, Berry's horse fell in with a party of about 100 cavalry, mainly from Lord Goring's Lifeguard, led by Lieutenant-Colonel James Dundas of Cleveland's Regiment, whom Hopton had sent out to scout. The Royalists had the worst of the skirmish and Dundas was mortally wounded and captured.

Hopton was already aware of Fairfax's advance, albeit by accident, thanks to a report from a young lieutenant of horse and eight of his troopers who had stumbled across the enemy during an unauthorised plundering expedition. The Royalist commander came to the conclusion that to abandon Torrington and retreat into Cornwall would at best only delay the final result: instead, it would be better to make a stand and give battle 'where I had some sort of cover for my foot, and opportunity to make good use of my horse.'

Torrington had a population of about 2,270 people. In 1579 the antiquarian John Leland had written: 'Torrington is a great large town and standeth on the brow of a hill and hath three fair streets in it.' These thoroughfares —Mill Street, Well Street and South Street — contained about 300 houses. The hill on which the town stood commanded two bridges crossing the River Torridge, carrying the roads leading to Cornwall. The remains of a castle that also overlooked the river were no longer of military significance. Torrington was a market town, with gardens and small enclosed fields on its outskirts and common land to the north and moors beyond.

It remains slightly unclear how many troops Hopton had with him. Clarendon estimated his strength at 6,800 men, but Hopton himself said that he had 3,300 horse and fewer than 2,000 foot. In any case, his men were of distinctly poorer quality than their opponents, and Hopton knew that his only hope lay in standing on the defensive.

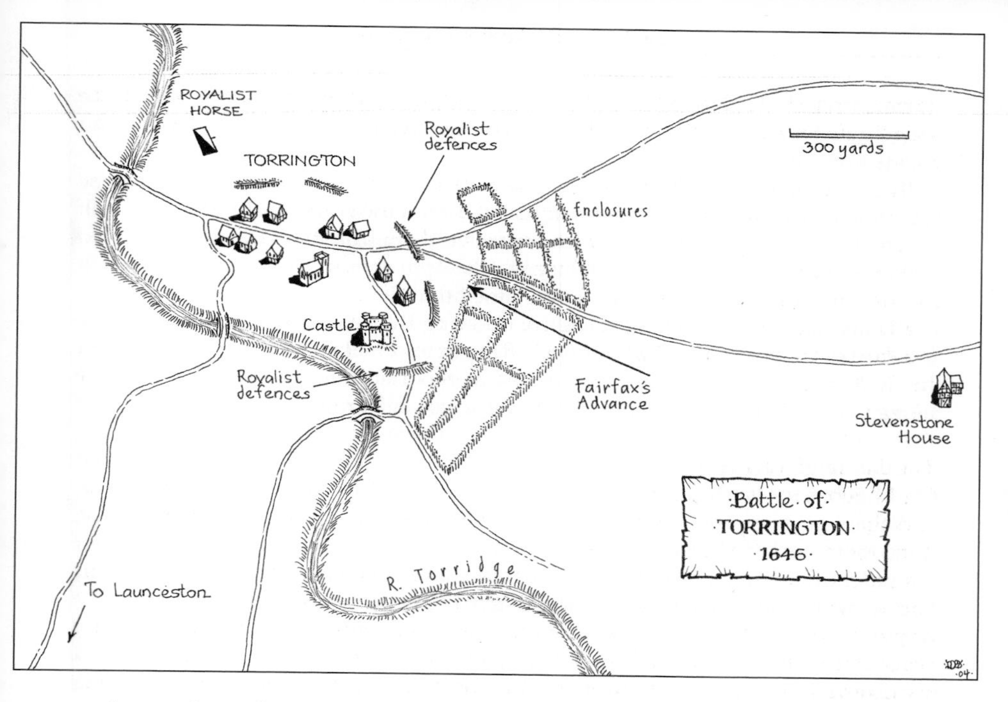

Attempting to hearten his men with reports that the King was marching to their support at the head of a victorious army, Hopton erected barricades of earth and felled trees at the entrances to the town. He manned these with his foot, backed with 200 horse divided into parties of 40, within the town, whilst the remainder of the cavalry, under Major-General Webbe, were kept in reserve on the common to the north of the town. Hopton also established an outpost of about 200 dragoons at Stevenstone House, about a mile to the east of the town.

Hopton's aim was to stand at Torrington long enough to force the enemy to withdraw through shortages of supplies, for, as Fairfax admitted in his despatch, 'if they could with all their force make good the Town, and put us to lie in the field, there being no villages near it that could shelter the Army, the wet weather continuing would have forced us to draw back and make our firearms little useful.'

A further problem for the Parliamentarians was that their supply line was much longer than that of their opponents, and subject to disruption by raiding Royalist cavalry and the garrison of Barnstaple. If Fairfax were forced to withdraw, lack of supplies would also probably compel him to abandon the siege of Exeter. Both sides were playing for high stakes.

However, in the morning of 16 February the weather seemed to be clearing and Sir Thomas resolved to gamble on the improvement lasting long enough for him to deal with Hopton. 'The drums beat by four of the clock in the morning' and the army was on the march by seven, now being about three miles from Torrington.

Fairfax's men trudged through the narrow lanes, led by a forlorn hope of horse under Major Stephens and Captain Molyneux. As they approached Stevenstone House the Royalist dragoons stationed there withdrew, losing a number of men in skirmishing in the lanes leading to Torrington. Some firing continued in the hedgerows for about two hours, the skirmishers 'exchanging coarse language and bullets now and then'.

By about 5 p.m. the bulk of Fairfax's men were drawn up 'in battalia' in Stevenstone Park, with the forlorn hope about half way between them and Torrington. The half dozen or so hedged enclosures which separated them from the town were manned by Royalist foot, with one field separating the opposing sides. As darkness fell, it was uncertain whether battle would be joined that day.

Fairfax planned to wait for daylight, ordering the 1,000 musketeers, 500 horse and fifty dragoons of the forlorn hope 'to stand and make good that ground until the next morning', but at about 8 p.m. it was reported that the Royalist foot were falling back into the town; an hour later, as Fairfax and Cromwell rode up to inspect their sentries, the sound of beating drums was heard within the town. Believing that this might signal the beginning of a Royalist withdrawal, Cromwell ordered the dragoons to 'steal up to the barricades to see what they were a-doing'. However, as Wogan's men approached the enemy defences, Hopton's musketeers, still in place, 'gave them such a volley, that they soon repented of their rashness.' Seeing their comrades under fire, 'our forlorn hope of foot... thought themselves bound in honour (for all the Lieutenant-General could say to the contrary) to help the dragoons . . .' Hopton had his troops in position, and 'it displeased me not at all that the enemy gave on, which he did that Monday night about 7 of the clock; about which time I with some of the General Officers of the horse got on horseback and placed the several parties of horse as before mentioned...'

It seems that the Parliamentarian Forlorn Hope had the worst of the first encounter and were beginning to give ground when Fairfax decided to launch a full-scale assault: 'being thus far engaged, the general . . . seeing the general resolution of the Soldiery, held fit, that the whole Regiments in order, after them should fall on, and so both sides were engaged, in the dark, for some two hours, till we beat them from the Hedges, and within the Barricades.'

The Parliamentarian field word was initially 'Emmanuel, God with us', and they wore a recognition sign of a furze bough in their hats. However, after the Royalists obtained knowledge of them from some prisoners, the word was changed to 'Truly' and the sign to a white handkerchief around hat or arm. The latter probably caused some confusion as the Royalists were also using a white handkerchief as their sign. Their word was 'We are with you.'

The main Royalist barricade was at the foot of Well Street, held by Cornish troops who, as the enemy approached, redoubled their rate of fire. Fierce fighting continued for over an hour, the Parliamentarians admitting that the Royalist foot 'disputed the entrance of our forces with push of Pike and butt end of Musket for a long time'. Eventually some of the Parliamentarian infantry, commanded by Robert Hammond, managed to outflank the barricades, infiltrating the town through the backs of some houses. However the fighting went on. Fairfax admitted that

> . . . our men were thrice repulsed by their Horse, and almost all driven out again, but Colonel Hammond with some other Officers and a few Soldiers made a stop at the Barricadoes [*sic*], and so making good their re-entrance,

rallied their men and went on again. Major Stephens with their Forlorn Hope of Horse coming seasonably up to second them, the Enemys' foot ran several ways . . . They [the Royalists] maintained the barricades, lines and hedges with as much resolution as could be expected, and had not our men gone on with extraordinary courage, they had been repulsed.

Hopton, on the other hand, condemned the performance of many of his troops:

About 8 of the clock that night, the Major General and myself in the street on horseback, and riding to visit the several posts, the enemy got entrance at the barricades at the upper end of the street where we were, and beat off the foot: and our party of horse that I had sent to support them ran away and fell down upon us, where the enemy being drawn up in a body in the street, and the Major General's horse being killed under him, I was therefore left with only Captain Harper and one of my servants engaged, but I thank God, got off with little hurt [a pike wound in the face] besides the loss of my horse, which brought me to my lodging door and there fell down dead, Captain Harper being shot in the head but not slain.

Meanwhile the parties of Royalist horse in Torrington fled 'and brought a confusion and disorder in the whole', whilst the foot, especially, according to Hopton the Cornish, also made off. An exception was the Prince of Wales' Regiment, which made a stand on the castle green and 'defended their post even after the town was lost.'

However the fight was not yet over. Many of the Parliamentarian foot scattered through the town in search of booty, and in the meantime Hopton had got another

The view eastwards along Well Street, where some of the fiercest fighting of the battle took place, as Fairfax's men forced the Royalist barricade.

horse and ridden off to the north end of Torrington, where the bulk of the Royalist horse were stationed, and

> . . . commanded my own Lieutenant-Colonel [Edward] Bovill with about 30 horse, and Lieutenant-Colonel Marsh, with my Lord of Cleveland's brigade, being about 5 or 600 horse, to draw up and charge into the town; my Lieutenant-Colonel to go first as the forlorn hope. At the same instant, there came to us about 300 of our musketeers that were fled out of the town, whom I commanded to join with them, but the foot presently ran away.

The Royalist counter-attack got as far as the barricades, where Hopton's men were again held, and as confused fighting continued the combatants were deafened by a tremendous explosion. The Royalists had established their main magazine, containing about eighty barrels of powder, in Torrington Church. When they first penetrated the town, the Parliamentarians had placed about 200 Royalist prisoners in the church. Although allegations of Royalist sabotage were made later by some Parliamentarian writers, it seems more likely that some gunpowder was ignited accidentally, probably by a carelessly smoking prisoner or guard. The detonation, of which one eyewitness said 'Hell itself could not make a more hideous sulphur', not only killed the prisoners and their guards but also wrecked the church and neighbouring houses and showered the streets with debris. Fairfax himself narrowly escaped being hit by a large piece of lead which killed one of his orderlies.

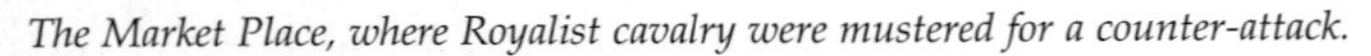

The Market Place, where Royalist cavalry were mustered for a counter-attack.

The Church of St Michael, rebuilt after the explosion.

The explosion caused general consternation, which ended the Royalist counter-attack but also assisted Hopton's horse in withdrawing from Torrington. They were further aided by the nature of the narrow, twisting street which led down to the River Torridge and hindered any concerted pursuit by the disorganised Parliamentarians. Hopton's cavalry, as well as large numbers of foot, succeeded in making their escape over the bridges and fords of the Torridge and retreated into Cornwall, the foot scattering over a wide area.

Torrington was a fatal blow for the Western Royalists. Although their casualties were not especially heavy — about sixty were killed in the actual fighting and another 200 in the church, with about 400 other prisoners taken — they had also lost about 1,600 weapons and most of their powder. More important was the blow to their morale. The New Model, which itself lost about 200 men, enlisted many of the Royalist prisoners in its ranks, whilst others were paroled and given 2s. apiece to return home, 'which it is hoped will prove of as good consequence to gain more of their affections as that civil useage [*sic*] was at Dartmouth.'

The End in the West

Fairfax was determined not to repeat the mistakes made by Essex and gave strict orders that any burning or plundering on entering Cornwall would be punished by death. When, on 24 February, the advance was resumed, the weather proved to be a greater hindrance than the Royalists. The 800 or so Royalist horse still in reasonable order fell back before the Parliamentarian advance, and Fairfax took Launceston without opposition. By the end of February all of the crossings of the Tamar were in Parliamentarian hands, and faint hopes that the Western Royalist horse might break out to join the King were at an end.

On 1 March, once again meeting no opposition from the dispirited Royalist horse, Fairfax occupied Bodmin. Many of the retreating Royalists were reportedly drunk, whilst many of the 400 or so foot still with Hopton were Welsh 'by the leeks in their hats and drink in their heads which caused a disorderly march. It being St Taffie's Day'.

Pendennis Castle, where diehard Royalists held out until August 1646. Its fall marked the end of the First Civil War in the West.

Fairfax had no wish to fight another action with the demoralised remnants of Hopton's troops and continued gently to herd them westwards, whilst the Royalist commanders accepted the inevitability of their defeat. By now increasing numbers of the Cornish gentry were making their own peace with Fairfax.

On 7 March the Royalist cavalry were defeated in a final skirmish as the Parliamentarians closed in on Truro and Hopton yielded to the inevitable. Placing his remaining reliable foot in the garrisons of Pendennis Castle and St Michael's Mount, on 9 March he asked Fairfax for a cessation of hostilities. On 16 March the remaining 4–5,000 horse and 3–4,000 foot of the Western Army surrendered on generous terms.

It only remained for Fairfax to mop up the remaining Royalist garrisons. Exeter surrendered on 13 April, three days after Barnstaple. Pendennis held out until 17 August, when its capitulation marked the end of the Civil War in the West.

BATTLEFIELD TOURS

Introduction

Several points may perhaps be usefully made before commencing our individual Battlefield Tours. At the time of writing (2004), of the battles discussed here, only Stratton, Lansdown and Roundway Down are reasonably well signposted and interpreted on site. Visits even to these, and still more to the others described, require both careful navigation and driving along typically high-banked and thick-hedged West Country roads, sometimes erratically signposted. As the author can testify from personal experience, becoming temporarily lost in the process is virtually inevitable from time to time. In order to minimise (but almost certainly not entirely remove) this irritant, would-be visitors are advised before setting out to study the appropriate sheet from the OS 1:25000 scale 'Explorer' series of maps (details are given with each tour), together with the suggestions given here, and plan their route in advance. In the tours described, all the grid references quoted relate to the OS 'Explorer' series.

Only Roundway Down of our examples has really adequate parking facilities. In the case of our other battles, limited informal parking can be found, but an exploration of virtually all of the battlefields requires some walking along lanes or more major roads which often carry a surprising volume of sometimes high-speed traffic. Great care should be exercised at all times.

A final caveat. At least part of all of our battlefields lie on private land. Bearing in mind the restrictions sometimes imposed by livestock and crops, landowners and farmers are generally co-operative in allowing responsible access to battlefield explorers. In return we should remember that our battlefields are often their workplaces, and observe the Country Code, particularly with regard to closing gates and keeping any accompanying dogs under close control.

TOUR ONE

Braddock Down

[O.S. 'Explorer' Sheet 107]

Braddock Down shares with Langport, and to a lesser extent Roundway Down, some debate over the exact location of the battle. Traditionally it was held to have been fought just to the south-west of Braddock Church. However, recent research by Rod Wilton, now accepted by the English Heritage Battlefields Register, suggests that the encounter actually took place further to the east, between the villages of Middle and East Taphouse, and this location is followed here.

A visit to Braddock Down can be conveniently included within a tour of the sites associated with the site of the Lostwithiel campaign of 1644. From Lostwithiel go east for about six miles along the A390 in the direction of Liskeard. At Middle Taphouse [SX174638] turn right along the B3359. Immediately beyond the hedges on your left is the initial position occupied by the Royalist forces. The tumulus near the junction with the A390 may be the 'hill' on which the Royalist guns were positioned.

Continue southwards along the B3359 for just over half a mile. On the right, immediately after passing a turning on the left into a minor road, there is a small informal parking place.

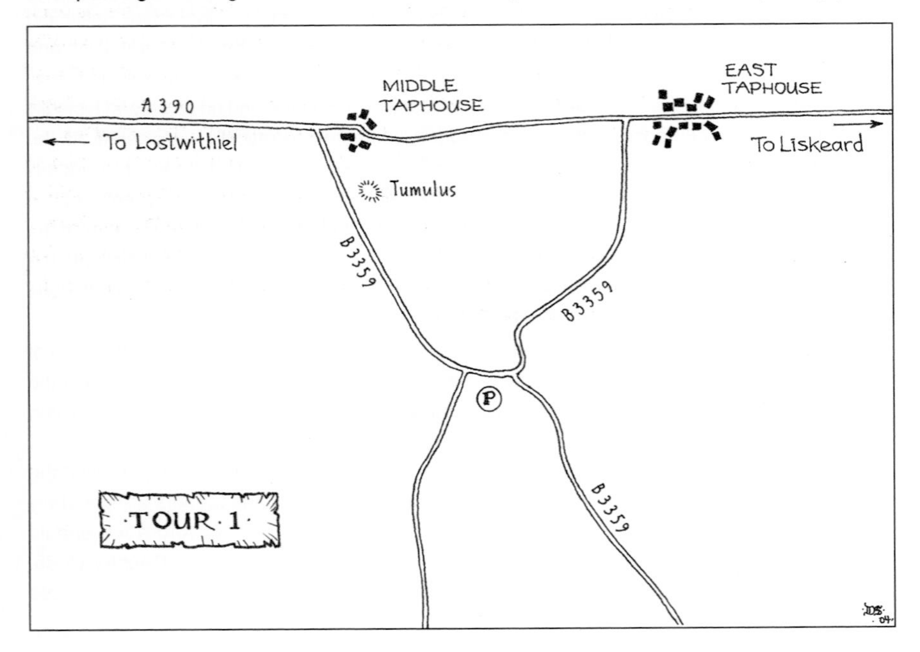

Braddock Church

From here, looking north, the best view of the field may be obtained. On the left is the rising ground occupied by Hopton. To the right is the ridge where Ruthven's Parliamentarians were positioned. The dip across which the Royalists attacked (now partly wooded) is clearly visible.

At the junction turn left, and return north, again along the B3359 (the roads on both sides of the battlefield somewhat confusingly have the same numbering). Largely obscured by hedges, Ruthven's position lies to your left. On reaching the A390, turn left to return to Lostwithiel.

For those wishing to inspect the traditional site of the battle, look out out for a minor road on the left, just under a mile in the Lostwithiel direction, signposted Braddock Church [SX153632] Continue along this lane for a mile, reaching Braddock Church. Immediately to the south-west of the church is the ridge which in this interpretation was held by the Parliamentarians. The corresponding ridge held by the Royalists about half a mile further to the south-west, and the intervening dip, is now thickly wooded and part of the Boconnoc estate.

TOUR TWO

Stratton

[O.S. 'Explorer' Sheet 111]

The actual battlefield is about half a mile north of Stratton village, with only limited informal parking by the roadside. However there is a free car park in Stratton itself, on the right hand side just after entering Stratton from the east along the A3072, and the battlefield is a reasonably easy 15–20 minute walk from there.

Walking through the village in a westerly direction, note on the right, just before crossing the bridge over the River Neet, the Tree Inn. This reputedly was Hopton's headquarters before the battle.

At the junction of the A3072 with the A39 turn right [SS228068]. Those on foot may wish to go directly ahead along a minor road through a housing estate. After a couple of hundred yards, this road bends to the right, with a public footpath turning off on the left hand side. Follow this across the fields for about a quarter of a mile. You are now on approximately the Royalist start line. The path now skirts woodland on the edge of Broomhill Manor [SS223072].

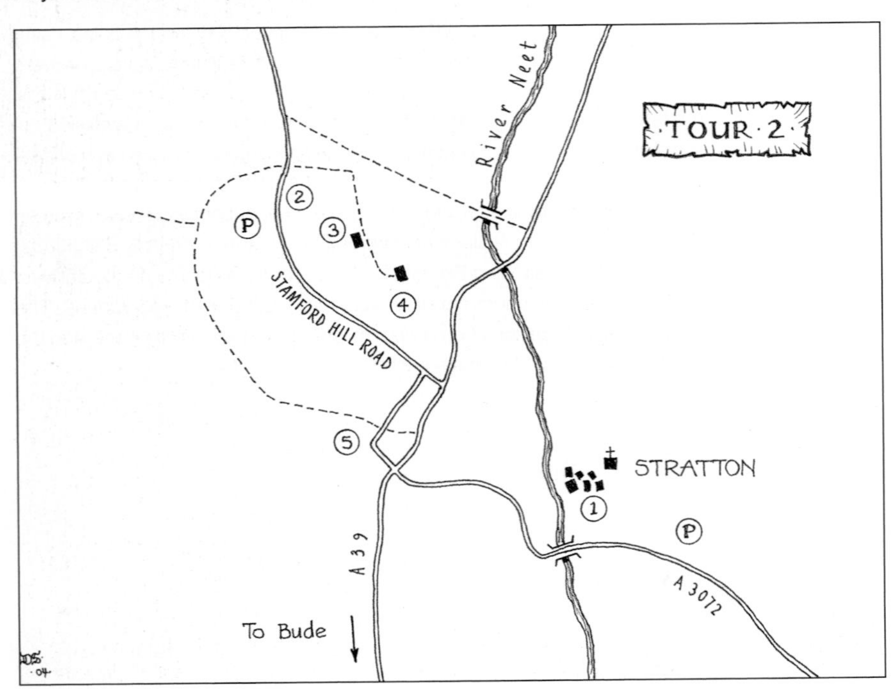

Where the path reaches a junction turn right and proceed eastwards uphill for about four hundred yards. You are now following the line of the Royalist attack. At the junction of the path with Stamford Hill Road, cross and look for a gate on the right hand side with a signboard indicating the Stratton Battlefield site. Go through this. Turning right, you are now on the summit of Stamford Hill, in the centre of the position held by the Parliamentarian forces. A useful interpretative panel here helps orientate the visitor and gives brief information about the battle. The earthwork on the summit may still be traced, and it now bears a commemorative plaque From here, proceed a few yards to your right to view the Monument in the grounds of Bevill House.

For those not wishing to undertake the field walk, at the junction in Stratton of the A3072 and A39 turn right, and after about two hundred yards left along

(Right and below) The monument on Stamford Hill.

Interpretation panels at Stamford Hill

Stamford Hill Road. The area is now partly built over, but surviving lanes and house driveways demonstrate the steepness of the ascent. In about a quarter of mile you will see the gate leading on to the summit of the hill and the battlefield to your right. Limited informal parking is possible on the verge nearby and a leaflet with a marked trail is available in the village

TOUR THREE

Lansdown

[O.S. 'Explorer' Sheet 155]

Lansdown, thanks to work carried out recently by the local authority, is by far the best interpreted of the battlefields described here. As usual, however, parking is limited.

The battle is best understood by following the line of the Royalist advance down from Freezing Hill. Proceeding westwards along the A420 from the direction of Marshfield, about half a mile west of its junction with the A46 turn left along Freezinghill Lane [ST733727]. Proceed southwards along this road. After about half a mile you are on the summit of Freezing Hill [ST725716], where the Royalists took up position prior to the battle. The road then crosses the valley where the initial fighting took place. Ahead of you are the slopes of Lansdown Hill. The road now bends right. Continue uphill past the junction on the right with another minor road, and, passing through trees, you are now following the probable route of Grenville's pikemen in their attack. Unfortunately the absence of verges on the road and the volume of fast-moving traffic make this section of the road highly dangerous to explore on foot.

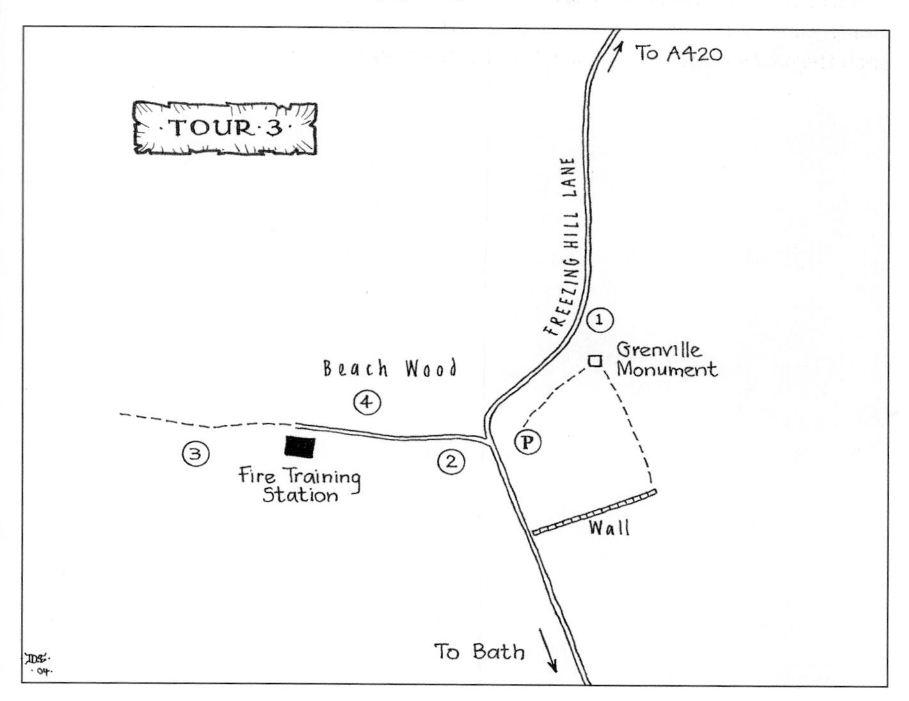

On reaching the relatively open plateau on the summit of the hill, a small informal parking area may be found on the left. Examine the useful interpretative panels and way marker here, then carefully cross the road to its western side and proceed on foot in a westerly direction along the Cotswold Way, which runs alongside a service road leading to a Fire Service Training Station, clearly distinguished by its wireless mast. Before entering the gate leading on to the Cotswold Way, look to your left across the service road. The area of hills and hollows, partly covered by scrub (2), probably represents the pits in which Royalist musketeers took cover in the closing stages of the battle. To your right the slope of Lansdown is partly concealed by the trees of Beach Wood (4) — possibly more extensive than in 1643 — which provided cover for Parliamentarian musketeers during the initial Royalist assault.

Carry on along the path, following the directional 'flags', past the Fire Brigade buildings until a gate leads you into open pasture land (3) . This is the end of the battlefield known as Hanging Hill, and from here there is a wide-reaching prospect which demonstrates the significance of Lansdown. Here too it is possible fully to appreciate the steepness of the ascent which the Royalists made, and the remains of a hollow way, perhaps one of the tracks used by Hopton's men, can be traced.

Retrace your steps to the road and parking area, taking a cautious look down the slope of Freezinghill Lane to your left, and make your way to the Grenville Monument (1), clearly visible

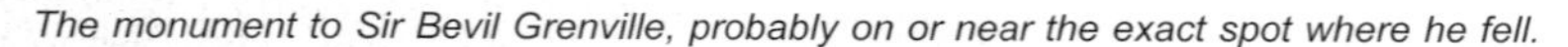

The monument to Sir Bevil Grenville, probably on or near the exact spot where he fell.

(Upper) Interpretation panels at Lansdown; and (lower) one of the way markers erected recently to denote the battlefield trail.

about a hundred yards away on the crest of the hill to the north-east. This probably marks, with a fair degree of accuracy, the place where Grenville fell mortally wounded. The whole of this plateau was the scene of the intense hand-to-hand fighting between the Royalist foot and Waller's horse.

Follow the Cotswold Way about a hundred yards eastward until it turns sharply south. At the junction of two paths follow the one on the right, leading back to the road. On your left note the stone wall and enclosure, which are almost certainly part of the walls which formed Waller's position at the end of the battle.

TOUR FOUR

Roundway Down

[O.S. 'Explorer' Sheet 157]

This is another battle the exact location of which has recently been the subject of some debate, the English Heritage Battlefields Register suggesting a site slightly further to the south than other versions. The argument is unlikely to be resolved unless a carefully planned search for artefacts is undertaken. However, all of the terrain likely to be involved can be covered in the course of a walk over rolling downs which provide far-reaching views of the whole area.

From Devizes take the A361 in the direction of Beckhampton [SU089695]. After passing the Hopton Industrial Estate [SU024631] on your left, about one mile further on take the first turning on your left and proceed across what is the battle area, past the golf course and park in the picnic area at Smallgrain Plantation (1) [SU029679].

Cross the picnic area diagonally and go down some steps on to a trackway, which marks the line of the Roman road to Bath. Turn right and join a path which runs along the Wansdyke, and carry on uphill past a wireless station on your left and continue along the Wansdyke for approximately half a mile until, after passing through a metal gate, a junction with another track is reached (2). This is the point where the old Marlborough–Bath road crossed the Wansdyke: the Royalist cavalry came on to the field and deployed to the left of you.

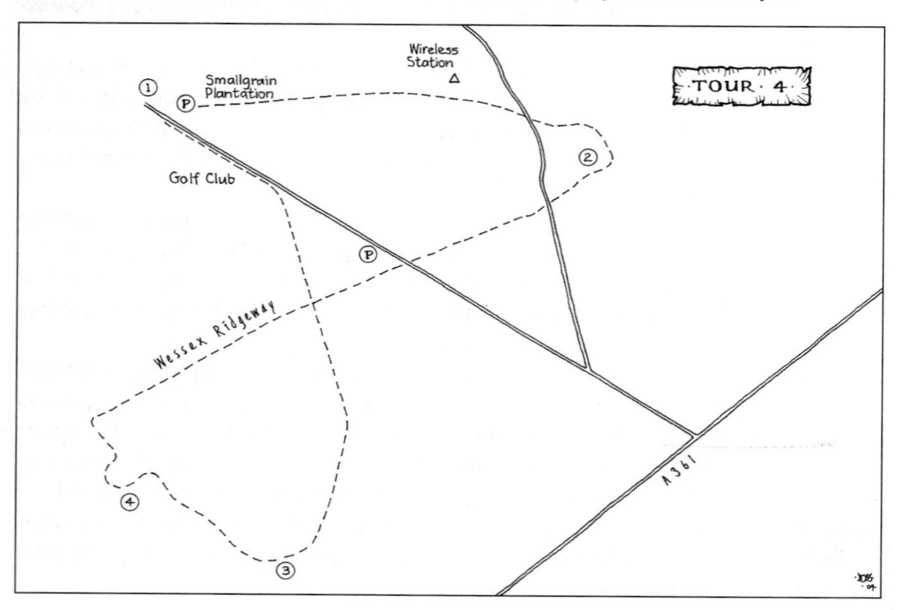

A view of the excellent terrain for cavalry over which the battle was fought.

Continue along the right hand track and straight on at the next junction towards the road. After about 350 yards go left and then cross the road. To your left front is the high ground where Waller was drawn up, with the 'Lobsters' on the left , foot in the centre and Waller and his own horse on the right.

At the next junction of tracks turn left and go steadily uphill about for one and a quarter miles to Roundway Hill (3). Most of the cavalry action took place on the slopes to your left. At Roundway Hill, note the steep descent southwards. Turn right through The Plantation and keep straight ahead with the fence to your right along a hedged track with a metalled road to your left. At the 'R6' waymarker go right for just under a mile along a hedged, metalled track to a junction. There is an interpretative panel about the battle a short distance along the track leading to the right.

After inspecting the panel go back to the junction on to the left-hand path and then immediately turn right. Skirt Roundway Hill Covert by the right hand path, noting on your left the precipitous slopes down which part at least of Waller's horse are said to tumbled (although the specific incident could have occurred at more than one location along Roundway Down's steep southern and western edges).

At Oliver's Castle earthworks (4) bear right and left at the next junction. On reaching a metalled track turn right past Hill Cottage. Note the height of King's Play Hill on your left. The track bends to the right and after about a quarter of a mile a junction is reached. Turn left here and follow the track diagonally past the golf club house. Turn left up the metalled road and follow it for about four hundred yards back to the car park.

This is a fairly lengthy and at times reasonably strenuous walk. A shorter route, covering the areas of likely fighting as identified by English Heritage, can be found by parking at a small informal pull-in just to the north-west of where the Wessex Ridgeway crosses the road. Keeping a close watch for traffic, walk back for about one hundred yards to the point where the trackways cross the road. Take the right hand (westerly) path, then follow the route given above as far as the junction in tracks where the first route turns left to the golf club. In this instance carry straight on and after about 300 yards find yourself back on the road at your starting point to the right of the small parking place.

TOUR FIVE

Lostwithiel

[O.S. 'Explorer' Sheet 107]

Covering as it does a campaign of several weeks involving a number of actions over a fairly wide are,a this is by far the longest of the tours. It is suggested that, in order to have time to visit all the relevant sites with sufficient time to appreciate them, the visitor should allow at least two days. A car — or bicycle for the more athletic — is essential. The town of Lostwithiel, with a good choice of accommodation and eating places, provides a convenient base of operations with a good deal more comfort than it afforded the Earl of Essex.

The first part of the tour covers sites associated with the opening phase of the campaign. Before setting out, however, the visitor may wish to note two locations within Lostwithiel itself relating to later in the fighting. The spire of St Bartholomew's Church (1) is still a prominent feature, bearing on its eastern side the scar resulting from the Parliamentarians' attempt to blow it up. On the eastern edge of the town the River Fowey is still crossed by the medieval Lostwithiel Bridge (2), which prompt action by the Royalists on 31 August prevented the Parliamentarians from demolishing. Note how closely the town is surrounded by overlooking high ground, possession of which was vital to the Royalists.

The next nearest location, within easy walking distance of Lostwithiel — about half a mile to the north of the town centre along Restormel Road — is Restormel Castle (3) , taken by Grenville's Cornish on 21 August. Now in the care of English Heritage, the Castle is well worth a visit.

Much of the earlier action in the campaign took place around Lanhydrock House (4) [SX088637]. Although almost entirely rebuilt after a major fire in the late nineteenth century, the House, now in the care of the National Trust, contains interesting material relating to the Robartes family and repays a visit. To reach it take the B3268 northwards out of Lostwithiel, and at its junction with the B3269 turn right. Lanhydrock is about a mile along on the right. At a junction with two minor roads a couple of hundred yards short of the A30 [SX082637], take the right-hand fork. Just beyond is a convenient parking area for visitors to Lanhydrock.

After visiting the House continue a short distance along the same road to the next junction [SX092643] and turn right, proceeding about half a mile until reaching a parking area near Respryn Bridge (5), captured by Grenville early in the campaign.

After inspecting the bridge, cross it and reach a fork about a hundred yards beyond. Both forks lead to the A390. If returning to Lostwithiel take the right hand fork and on reaching the A390 turn right. This might, however, be a suitable opportunity to end the day with a visit the Braddock Down battlefield. In this case take the left hand fork and on reaching the A390 turn left and follow the directions given in the Braddock Down Tour.

It is recommended that a second day be devoted to visiting sites connected with the later stages of the campaign. From Lostwithiel take the A390 in the direction of Liskeard. After about a quarter of a mile take a minor road on the right [SX119598] and almost immediately turn left

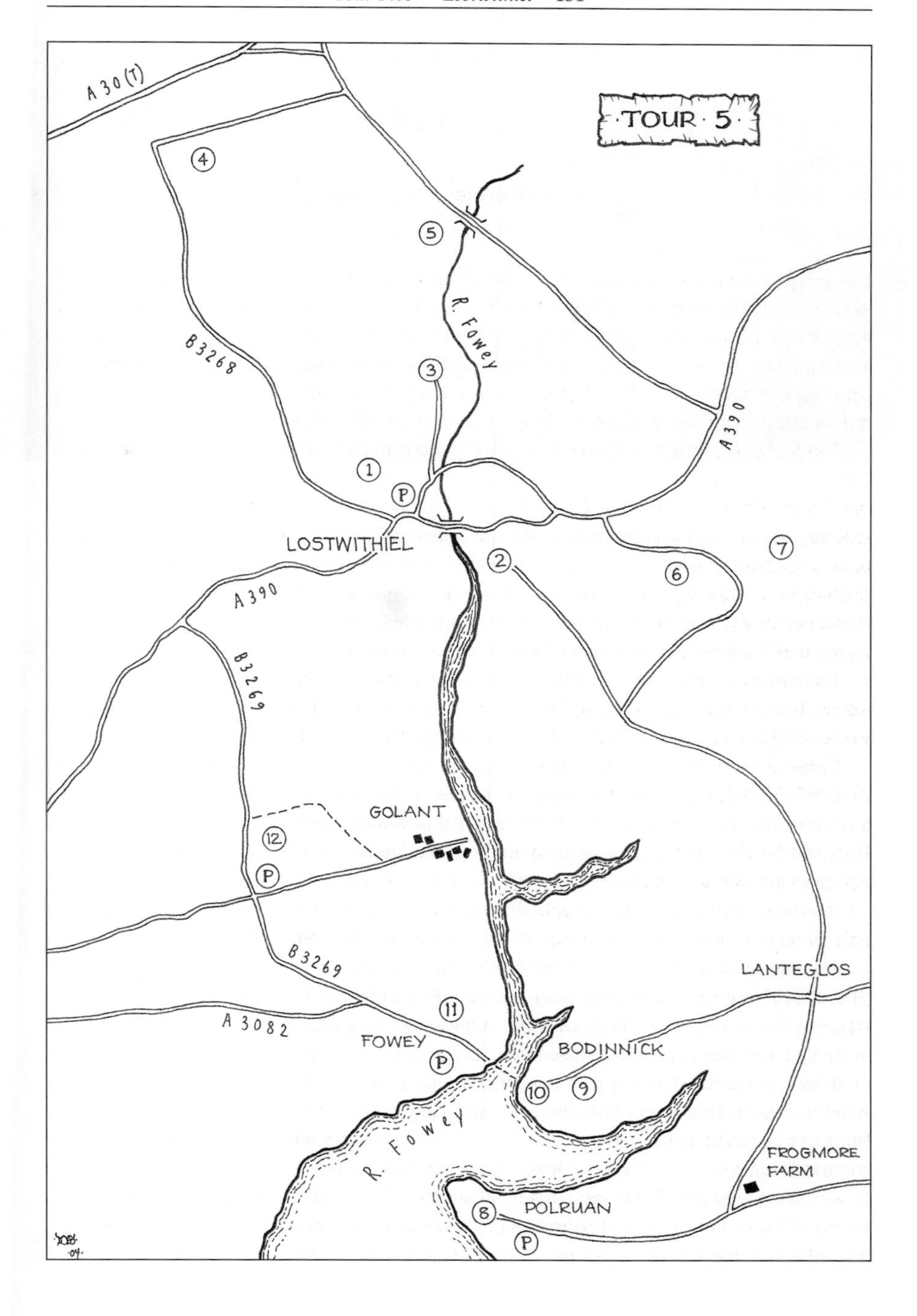

TOUR 5
A 30 (T)
4
5
R. Fowey
B3268
3
A390
1
P
LOSTWITHIEL
2
7
6
A390
B3269
GOLANT
12
P
B3269
LANTEGLOS
11
A 3082
FOWEY
P
BODINNICK
10
9
R. Fowey
FROGMORE
FARM
8
POLRUAN
P

Fowey from Polruan.

up a narrow ascending lane. Beacon Hill (6), which was vital to the possession of Lostwithiel, is about 300 yards along on your right. Parking is possible, with some care, along the verge of the lane. The summit of the Hill is on farmland, and although access, via a field gate, is usually permitted, visitors should exercise due consideration, and also be aware of a disused mineshaft located on the western slope of the Hill to the right. Follow a hedge on your left to the summit, from where the dominating location of Beacon Hill is clearly apparent. The high ground to the north-east of Lostwithiel is clearly visible, and the now wooded slopes of Druids Hill which were occupied by the Royalists early in the campaign are directly behind you.

Returning to the road, continue a hundred yards to a junction. Opposite is a track leading to the Cross and cottage marking the site of St Nectan's Chapel (7), around which Prince Maurice's foot were stationed at the start of the battle of Beacon Hill. In the woods to the north-east is Boconnoc House, the headquarters of King Charles during this phase of the campaign; it is not open to the public.

Returning down the track to the road junction, turn right and continue straight on along a narrow lane (beware of oncoming traffic) for about three-quarters of a mile until reaching a crossroads at Trewether Farm [SX119585]. Turn left here and follow the signs to Lerryn [SX142672]. From here follow the lanes southwards via Middle and Lower Penpoll to Lanteglos, then about a mile and a half further south to the road junction at Frogmore Farm [SX158517]. Turn right here and continue towards Polruan [SX127507].

There is restricted vehicle access to the village, so it is best to park in one of the two car parks and continue on foot down towards the quay. The main point of interest is the Fort or Blockhouse (8) at the tip of the peninsula. Occupied by the Royalists in August, this provided a site for a battery which closed off the entrance to Fowey harbour for Parliamentarian shipping. From the Fort the remains of the corresponding fort which formerly stood on the Fowey side, enabling the harbour mouth to be closed off by means of a chain, can be seen. This fort does not appear to have played any part in the 1644 campaign.

Passengers on foot may cross from Polruan to Fowey by means of a ferry, but visitors with a car should retrace their route out of Polruan for about a quarter of a mile. Where the road forks [SX13509] take the left hand option and continue for a mile along the wooded side of the inlet known as Pont Pill as far as the village of Pont [SX144525]. Turn left in the centre of the village, and left again at the next junction along the lane signposted Bodinnick. After three hundred yards take the first turning on the left: where the lane bends there is a short track leading to Hall Farm(9), formerly the residence of, and visited by, Charles I during his inspection the Royalist outpost at Bodinnick when he was narrowly missed by a cannon shot from the Fowey side.

Continue down into Bodinnick (10), where a car ferry will take you over to Fowey (although lengthy waits may be expected in summer).

Fowey itself was spared fighting during the campaign but remains a picturesque old town full of interest. Worthy of special mention in our connection are the Ship Inn, in the seventeenth-century home of the Royalist Rashlegh family and reportedly Essex's headquarters for part of the campaign (11), and the heavily restored Place House (not open to the public) which was the home of the prominent local Treffrey family.

Leave Fowey by the A3082 and continue for about half a mile. Just outside the town on the right hand side is the Tristan Stone, a fifth-century monument bearing the name of Arthurian fame.

At its junction with the A3082 [SX109525] go right along the B3269. We are now moving towards the scene of the fighting on 31 August 1644: the Parliamentarian baggage train around which Skippon mustered his troops prior to their surrender was probably drawn up somewhere in this area. After a mile the B3269 crosses two minor lanes [SX104546]. Park either at the crossroads or at a small informal pull-in just beyond and proceed northwards up the B3269 for about three hundred yards. Immediately before reaching a track leading off to the right towards Lawhibbet Farm, go through a gate on your right and directly in front of you are the remains of Castle Dor (12), with a memorial plaque commemorating the action of 31 August. The still substantial remains of the earthwork, forming the centre of the Parliamentarian line that day, provide a good vantage point from which to look along to the east, across the ground held and

Remains of Fowey blockhouse.

The view across the harbour to Bodinnick.

abandoned by Colonel John Weare's Foot, and northwards, towards the ground from which the Royalists advanced. A footpath leading along the lane in front of Castle Dor and through Lawhibbet Farm then turns south across the right flank of the Parliamentarian position and on to the lane running from Castle Dor to Golant [SX123547]. Turn right to go back to the crossroads at Castle Dor.

Continue northwards along the B3269. The countryside, with its rolling terrain and small hedged and banked fields, is little changed from 1644, when it saw a series of Royalist attacks and Parliamentarian counter-attacks during the advance on 31 August towards Castle Dor. Just before reaching Pelyn Wood [SX097576] take the lane which forks off to the right. This will take you back to Lostwithiel, and seems very likely to have been the muddy track in which some of Essex's guns were bogged down and abandoned on the morning of 31 August.

TOUR SIX

Langport

[O.S. 'Explorer' Sheet 129]

Langport is another battle whose exact site has been the subject of some debate in recent years. My own preference is for the site currently favoured by English Heritage and described here. The English Heritage Battlefields Register (see website in Bibliography) summarises the arguments for the three options.

Leave Langport by the B 3153 and after about half a mile reach Picts Hill (1) [ST434275]. The lane on the left provides a small informal parking area just beyond the row of houses on the right. You are now on the right of the position on Ham Down occupied by Goring's horse. To the east, beyond the hedgerows, the fields occupied by the Royalist musketeers at the start of the action can be see, with the ground sloping down towards the Wagg Rhyne, marked by line of small trees and rising beyond to the Parliamentarian positions on Pitney Hill.

Crossing the B3153, a path runs past a poultry farm to the railway, across the portion of Ham Down occupied at the start of the action by Goring's centre and right. Returning to the B3153, proceed (with care if on foot) eastwards down the slope to the Wagg Bridge(2). This is the lane up which Bethell's horse made their charge, and is still hedged on both sides. Reaching the post-1645 Wagg Bridge — which probably occupies the site of the ford — look back towards Ham Down to see the Royalist position from the perspective of the attacking Parliamentarian horse.

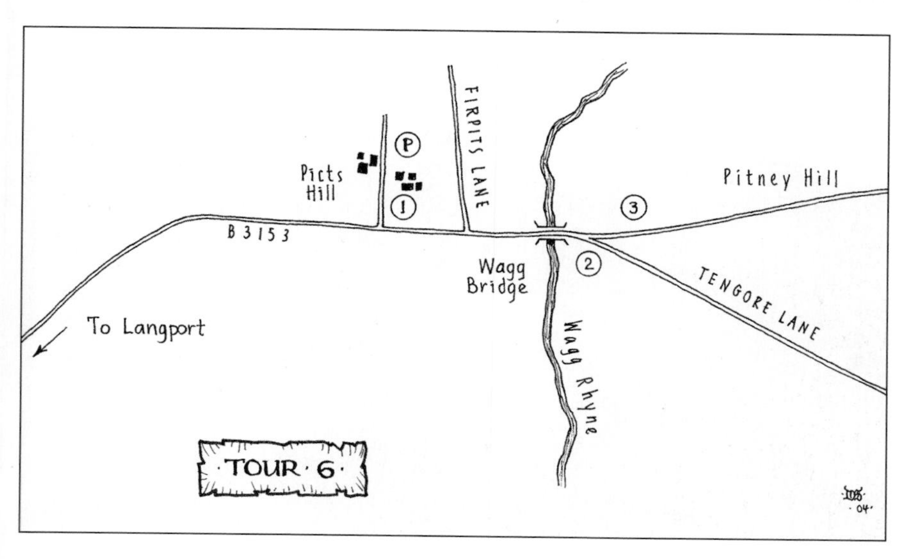

(Above) Castle Dor memorial plaque.

(Above) Wagg Bridge and (below) the Wagg Rhynne.

TOUR SEVEN

Torrington

[O.S. 'Explorer' Sheet 126]

Though Torrington is a pleasant market town, not many buildings remain that date from the time of the battle in 1646. However, the street plan is substantially the same, and the course of the battle for the town may be followed on the ground. Enter Torrington from the A386 Bideford–Barnstaple road via Whites Lane, at the end of which is a car park. This is convenient for the excellent 'Torrington 1646' Exhibition (1), which narrates the events of the battle with various other 'living history' features and provides a valuable introduction to a tour.

From here walk along South Street and turn left up Cornmarket Street to its junction with Well Street (2). The latter was barricaded by the Royalists and saw some of the heaviest fighting of the battle.

Turn right along Fore Street into the Market Place (3), noting the Black Horse Inn, which was the headquarters of Fairfax after the battle. At the end of Fore Street a passage leads to St Michael's Church, rebuilt after the explosion at the end of the battle. A cobbled mound near the main entrance to the Church reputedly marks the mass grave of those killed in the explosion.

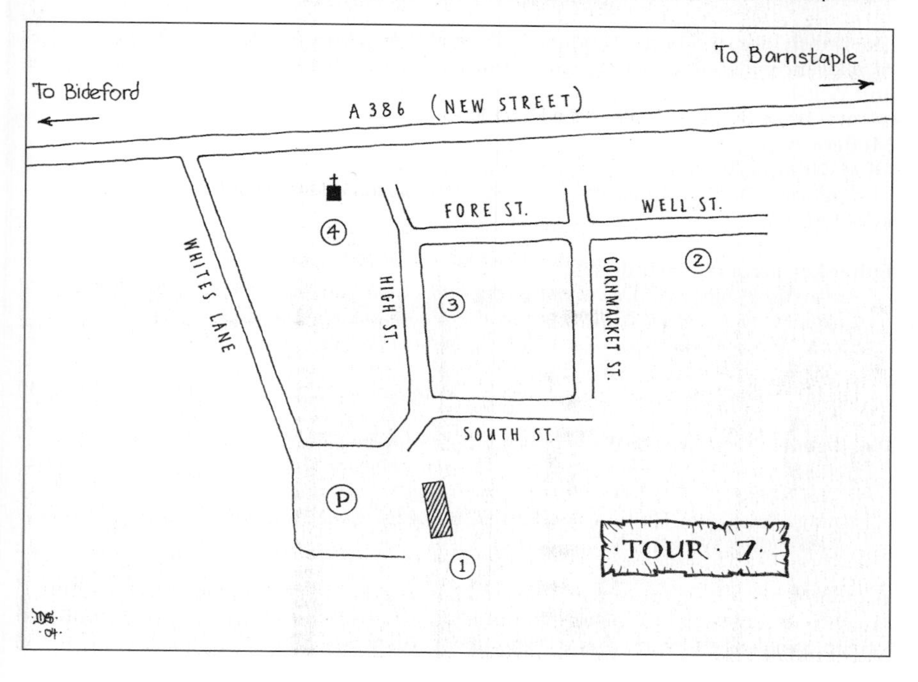

Select Bibliography

Primary Sources

Information about the Civil War in the South-West can be found in a vast range of contemporary sources, many of which are quoted in this book. Among the most important printed sources are:

Atkyns, Richard, 'The Vindication of Richard Atkyns', in *Military Memoirs: The Civil War* (ed. Peter Young), London, 1967.

Clarendon, Edward Earl of, *History of the Great Rebellion* (ed. W. D. Macray), Oxford, 1888.

Hopton, Lord Ralph, 'Bellum Civile', in *Transactions of the Somerset Record Society* (ed. C. E. H. Chadwick-Healey), Vol. 18, 1902.

Sprigge, Joshua, *Anglia Rediviva*, London, 1647. The 'official history' of the campaigns of the New Model Army in 1645–46).

Symonds, Richard, *Diary of the Marches of the Royal Army* (ed. C. E. Long), Camden Society, 1859.

Walker, Sir Edward, *Historical Discourses upon Several Occasions*, London, 1705.

The British Library, London, and the Bodleian Library, Oxford, contain major collections of relevant material, as do the County Records Offices of Cornwall, Devon, Somerset and Wiltshire as well as major libraries such as those at Exeter, Bristol and Truro.

Modern Accounts

Of major importance is the series of pamphlets dealing with almost every engagement of significance in the war published by Stuart Peachey of Historical Management Associates Ltd.

Other key accounts include:

Andriette, Eugene A., *Devon and Exeter in the Civil War*, Newton Abbott, 1971.

Coate, Mary, *Cornwall in the Great Civil War and Interregnum*, Oxford, 1933.

Stoyle, Mark, *West Britons: Cornish Identities and the Early Modern British State*, Exeter, 2002.

Underdown, David, *Somerset in the Civil War and Interregnum*, Newton Abbott, 1973.

Good general accounts of the war as a whole may be found in:

Reid, Stuart, *All the King's Armies: A Military History of the English Civil War, 1641–1651*, Staplehurst, 1998

Young, Peter, and Holmes, Richard, *The English Civil War: a Military History of the Three Civil Wars, 1642–51*, London, 1974.

A more recent excellent source of information is the English Heritage website (http://english-heritage.org.uk/filestore/battlefields), whose Battlefields Register contains valuable analyses of many of the engagements discussed here.

Index